Fundamentals in Agriculture Technology

भाकृअनुप
ICAR
Indian Council of Agricultural Research (ICAR)

Dr. Balasaheb Sawant Konkan Krishi Vidyapeeth (DBSKKV)

NAHEP
National Agricultural Higher Education Project-Institutional Development Plan (NAHEP-IDP)

nipa
NIPA® Genx Electronic Resources & Solutions P. Ltd., New Delhi-110 034

About the Authors

Shri Chintan Oza, Founder, Anantam Ecosystems, Regional Director, Founder Institute, Member, IISEC at IEEE TEMS, India Region Lead at IEEE Entrepreneurship.

Chintan is a serial entrepreneur with 23 years of experience in the telecom and ICT sectors. He is an alumnus of IIT Mumbai, UC Berkeley, and Oxford University, and holds a certification in Innovation and Technology Commercialization from Georgia Tech.

Chintan is currently the local leader of the Founder Institute in Mumbai and the Regional Director for India. He has worked with over 380 entrepreneurs across six continents, helping them with go-to-market strategies and scaling up their technology.

Chintan is also an active volunteer at several organizations, including the Project Management Institute, IEEE Technology Engineering Management Society, IEEE Entrepreneurship, Bombay Management Association, OneQuantum, Emerging Technologies Forum, Stanford Seed, Indian Chamber of International Business, and Rotary International.

He is on the advisory boards of several startups and academic institutions, and he has been an angel investor in three startups. He is also part of the investment committee for various venture capital funds, and collaborates with investment syndicates and angel investors. He is also an adjunct faculty member and a member of the advisory board at various academic institutions.

Chintan co-founded Arnima Energy Solutions, which is gearing up to launch a range of electric vehicles and high-speed chargers. He is also the India Region Lead for IEEE Entrepreneurship and is organizing a series of virtual events on the theme of protecting innovation.

Mr. Yogesh Harishchandra Naik, Consultant, Agri-input Industry and Director, AshtaLakshmi EnviroCare Services (29+ years of experience in Agro Input Marketing and Landscape Gardening & Corporate Cosmetic Maintenance | M. Sc. (Agri.) in Horticulture, Konkan Krishi Vidyapeeth, Dapoli, Dist. Ratnagiri, Maharashtra | M.A. - Leadership Science at Chanakya International Institute of Leadership Studies, University of Mumbai

Educational Qualification:

- B. Sc. (Agriculture): (1989) Konkan Krishi Vidyapeeth, Dapoli, Dist Ratnagiri, M.S.
- M. Sc. (Agriculture): (1991) Konkan Krishi Vidyapeeth, Dapoli, Dist Ratnagiri, M.S. with specialization in Horticulture (University Topper with C.G.P.A. 4.00 out of 4.00)

- Post Graduate Diploma in Marketing & Sales Management (1996) Bharatiya Vidya Bhavans, Chowpatty, Mumbai
- Post Graduate Diploma in Marketing & Advertising Management (1997) Bharatiya Vidya Bhavans, Chowpatty, Mumbai (Topper in the Institute)
- Diploma in Import & Export Management (2004) Welingkar Institute of Management (WE School), Matunga, Mumbai
- MA – Leadership Science (2021) Chanakya International Institute of Leadership Studies, University of Mumbai, Kalina Campus, Mumbai

Awards & Medals

- Awarded two Gold Medals for standing First in the University in M. Sc. (Agri.) degree Program

  Konkan Krishi Vidyapeeth - Gold Medal

  Hexamer Foundation - Gold Medal
- Awarded special "Golden Jubilee Award" from "Horticultural Society of India" for standing first in the University in M. Sc. (Agri.) degree in Horticulture
- Awarded "Green Advertising Gold Medal" & "NEIF Silver Medal" for standing First in the Institute in "P.G. Diploma in Marketing & Advertising"

Fundamentals in Agriculture Technology

Compiled by

Prashant S. Bodake
Dean & Director of Instruction, DBSKKV
Co-ordinator & Principal Investigator
NAHEP-IDP, DBSKKV-Dapoli, Maharashtra

Srinivasan Iyengar
Director of Jamnalal Bajaj Institute of Management Studies
Mumbai, Maharashtra

Santosh V. Sawardekar
Co- Principal Investigator
NAHEP-IDP, DBSKKV-Dapoli, Maharashtra

Authors

Chintan Oza
(Head), Founder, Anantam Ecosystems, Mumbai, Maharashtra

Yogesh Naik
Alumnus of DBS Konkan Krishi Vidyapeeth, Dapoli
Director, Ashta Lakshmi Enviro Care Services, Mumbai, Maharashtra

Indian Council of Agricultural Research (ICAR)

Dr. Balasaheb Sawant Konkan Krishi Vidyapeeth (DBSKKV)

National Agricultural Higher Education Project-Institutional Development Plan (NAHEP-IDP)

NIPA® Genx Electronic Resources & Solutions P. Ltd., New Delhi-110 034

Citation: National Agriculture Higher Education Project Institutional Development Plan, DBSKKV, Dapoli & ICAR, New Delhi

NIPA® GENX ELECTRONIC RESOURCES & SOLUTIONS P. LTD.

101,103, Vikas Surya Plaza, CU Block
L.S.C.Market, Pitam Pura, New Delhi-110 034
Ph : +91 11 27341616, 27341717, 27341718
E-mail: newindiapublishingagency@gmail.com
Website: www.nipabooks.com

For customer assistance, please contact
Phone: + 91-11-27 34 17 17
Fax: + 91-11-27 34 16 16

ISBN: 978-93-58871-12-8

Composed and Designed by NIPA®.

भारतीय कृषि अनुसंधान परिषद
कृषि अनुसंधान भवन–II, नई दिल्ली–110012
INDIAN COUNCIL OF AGRICULTURAL RESEARCH
KRISHI ANUSANDHAN BHAVAN-II, PUSA, NEW DELHI-110012
Phone: +91-11-25841760
Email: ddg.edu@icar.gov.in, ddgedn@gmail.com, nd.nahep@icar.gov.in

Dr. Rakesh Chandra Agrawal
Deputy Director General (Agril. Edn.)

Message

It is with immense pleasure and a sense of purpose that I provide this forward to the National Agricultural Higher Education Project-Institutional Development Plan (NAHEP-IDP) at Dr. Balasaheb Sawant Konkan Krishi Vidyapeeth (DBSKKV) and the concurrent endeavour to develop a short pilot course in skilling small-scale agri-entrepreneurship. This transformative initiative is under the guidance and leadership of the Hon'ble Vice Chancellor of DBSKKV Dr. S.G. Bhave.

Principal Investigator of NAHEP-IDP, DBSKKV-Dapoli Dr. P.S.Bodake, a distinguished and visionary leader in the field of agriculture, has consistently championed the cause of advancing agricultural education, research, and extension services. His strategic vision has played a pivotal role in shaping the trajectory of agricultural development in our nation, with a keen focus on empowering farming communities and fostering innovation.

The NAHEP-IDP of DBSKKV stands as a testament to ICAR & World Bank commitment to elevating the standards of agricultural education. By providing institutional support and promoting excellence across various facets of academia, research, and extension activities, the project aims to position DBSKKV as a center of excellence in agricultural learning and research.

In tandem with the NAHEP-IDP, the initiation of a short pilot course in skilling smallscale agri-entrepreneurship reflects DBSKKV foresight in addressing contemporary challenges in agriculture. Recognizing the pivotal role played by small-scale agri-entrepreneurs in driving rural economies, this course is designed to equip them with the necessary skills and knowledge to navigate the dynamic landscape of agribusiness.

The NAHEP-IDP, DBSKKV envisions this pilot course as a stepping stone toward fostering a culture of entrepreneurship in agriculture. By blending theoretical insights with practical applications, the course seeks to empower agri-entrepreneurs, enabling them to adopt sustainable farming practices, embrace innovation, and contribute significantly to the economic prosperity of their communities.

I extend my heartfelt appreciation to Dr. P.S. Bodake and his entire NAHEP-IDP Team for their steadfast leadership and unwavering commitment to advancing agricultural education and entrepreneurship. Under his guidance, these initiatives are poised to make a lasting impact on the agricultural education landscape and the entrepreneurial spirit within the students and farming community.

(R.C. Agrawal)
Deputy Director General (Agril. Edn.)

DR. BALASAHEB SAWANT KONKAN KRISHI VIDYAPEETH
Dapoli, Dist. Ratnagiri - 415712
Tel. No.: (0)02358-282064, **Fax No.**: 02358-282074, **Mob.**: 9422556565
E-mail : vcdbskkv-mh@gov.in, ipmbhave@gmail.com, **website** : www.dbskkv.org

Dr. Sanjay G. Bhave
IDP Leader
Vice Chancellor, DBSKKV

Message

I am delighted to present the Institutional Development Plan as part of the National Agricultural Higher Education Project (NAHEP) undertaken by our esteemed institution. This initiative marks a significant milestone in our commitment to advancing agricultural education, research, and innovation, with the ultimate goal of transforming the agricultural landscape of our nation.

This pilot course serves as a testament to our university's dedication to fostering innovation and fostering collaboration between academia and industry. We believe that by offering this course, we are not only contributing to the skill development of individuals but also playing a pivotal role in shaping the future of agriculture.

We at DBSKKV are happy to felicitate the proficient attainment of the Principal Investigator, IDP Coordinator, and Dean and Director of Instruction of DBSKKV-Dr.Prashant S. Bodake and team NAHEP-IDP involved in the same vertical. Your magnificent work makes all of us highly gratified and prosperous. Well Done!

I extend my gratitude to the faculty members, industry experts, and stakeholders who have contributed their expertise and insights to the development of this course. Their collective efforts have ensured that the curriculum aligns with the ever-changing demands of the agricultural sector.

I am excited to witness the impact that this short pilot course on skilling small-scale agricultural entrepreneurship will have on our participants and, consequently, on the agricultural landscape. With this initiative, we are sowing the seeds of empowerment and innovation, cultivating a new generation of agripreneurs who will not only navigate challenges but also unearth opportunities for growth.

(Sanjay G. Bhave)
IDP Leader
Vice Chancellor, DBSKKV

NATIONAL AGRICULTURAL HIGHER EDUCATION PROJECT
AGRICULTURAL EDUCATION DIVISION
INDIAN COUNCIL OF AGRICULTURAL RESEARCH
(Department of Agricultural Research and Education
Ministry of Agriculture and Farmers Welfare, Government of India)
Room No. 514, Krishi Anusandhan Bhawan-II, Pusa, New Delhi-110 012

Date : 14.12.2023

Dr. N.K. Jain
National Coordinator (IDP)

Message

It is a matter of great pleasure to learn that Dr. Balasaheb Sawant Konkan Krishi Vidyapeeth, Dapoli has developed short pilot course on “Skilling Small-scale Agri-Entrepreneurship” for the undergraduate students. The efforts made by DBSKKV, Dapoli and the Knowledge Experts is a significant stride towards fostering interdisciplinary learning and preparing students for the evolving landscape of agriculture. Agriculture, the backbone of our nation, is undergoing a transformative phase that demands a comprehensive understanding of not only traditional farming practices but also entrepreneurial skills. In this context, DBSKKV, Dapoli is driven by the vision to equip undergraduate students with the knowledge and skills necessary to navigate the complexities of modern agriculture and contribute to the burgeoning field of agri-entrepreneurship. I commend the leadership of Dr. S.G. Bhave, Hon’ble Vice Chancellor, DBSKVV, Dapoli for his forward-thinking approach in embracing this initiative and commitment to provide a robust academic environment aligns seamlessly with our objective of preparing students for the dynamic and competitive landscape of agriculture and entrepreneurship.

I also congratulate Dr. P.S. Bodake, Principal Investigator of NAHEP-IDP, DBSKKV, Dapoli and his entire team, whose collaborative efforts have been instrumental in shaping the curriculum of this course. Together, we envision a program that not only imparts knowledge but also nurtures a spirit of inquiry and enterprise among the students. I extend my warmest congratulations to the University on the launch of the innovative short pilot course on “Skilling Small-scale Agri-Entrepreneurship”. May this endeavour be a beacon of progress, fostering excellence in agricultural education and empowering the next generation of agri-entrepreneurs. University’s commitment to bridging theory and practical is commendable, and I am confident that this initiative will contribute significantly to the growth of our agricultural landscape.

Place: New Delhi

(N. K. Jain)

NATIONAL AGRICULTURE HIGHER EDUCATION PROJECT INSTITUTIONAL DEVELOPMENT PLAN
DR. BALASAHEB SAWANT KONKAN KRISHI VIDYAPEETH,
DAPOLI, DIST. RATNAGIRI
Mob. No.: 9420413255 / 8275201130
Email.: (P)prameghash@gmail.com (O) hodagrodapoli@gmail.com (O) piidpdbskkv@gmail.com (O)nodalcelldbskkv@gmail.com

Dr. P. S. Bodake
Dean & Director of Instruction
Coordinator, Principal Investigator, NAHEP-IDP

Message

It is with immense pride and anticipation that I present the Institutional Development Plan as part of our active involvement in the National Agricultural Higher Education Project (NAHEP). This plan embodies our institution's unwavering commitment to redefining agricultural education and research, and it signifies a transformative journey towards excellence and innovation.

Through this plan, we aim to enhance our institutional capacities, bolster research initiatives, and cultivate strategic partnerships with industries and communities. By incorporating modern pedagogical techniques, fostering interdisciplinary collaboration, and harnessing the potential of emerging technologies, we strive to create a learning ecosystem that empowers our students to become leaders and change-makers in the agricultural sector and it will not only elevate our institution's stature but also propel the agricultural education and research landscape towards a brighter and more sustainable future.

Our joint commitment to education and empowerment has culminated in the creation of this pilot course. Through a harmonious blend of theoretical insights and practical experiences, participants will delve into market trends, value chain analysis, sustainable practices, financial management, and the integration of technology into agriculture. This holistic approach is designed to prepare individuals to navigate the intricacies of agripreneurship with confidence.

This pilot course is an embodiment of our dedication to fostering collaboration between academia and industry. By bridging the gap between theory and practice, we aim to nurture a new generation of agripreneurs who are poised to steer the agricultural sector towards innovation and growth.

We sincerely mention primitive gratitude towards the former Vice-chancellor of DBSKKV Dr. Sanjay D. Sawant and Vice-chancellor of DBSKKV Dr. Sanjay G. Bhave for such prudent leadership and providence. We feel proud to highlight the sheer hard work and great dedication of the Co-Principal Investigator of NAHEP-IDP and IDP Staff.

We are grateful to the Director of Jamnalal Bajaj Institute of Management-Mumbai Dr. Shrinivasan Iyengar for such excellent association and cordial congruence in the course of developing a short pilot course in skilling small-scale Agri-Entrepreneurship. We also express our sincere gratitude to the faculty members of JBIMS & University of Mumbai, industry experts, and stakeholders whose expertise and contributions have shaped this course. Their collective wisdom ensures that the curriculum remains attuned to the evolving demands of the agricultural landscape.

Thank you.

(P. S. Bodake)
Dean & Director of Instruction
Coordinator, Principal Investigator, NAHEP-IDP

Preface

In the rapidly evolving landscape of agriculture, the infusion of technology has become a pivotal force shaping the future of farming practices. This book delves into the fundamentals of Agriculture Technology, with a specific focus on two transformative elements: Blockchain and Drones. As authors, we aim to provide a concise yet comprehensive exploration of these technological frontiers, shedding light on their role in revolutionizing agriculture practices.

The integration of Blockchain in agriculture marks a paradigm shift in how we perceive and manage the agri-food supply chain. In this section, we embark on a journey to unravel the potential of Blockchain technology and its profound impact on the agricultural sector. We begin by demystifying the intricate concepts of Blockchain, providing readers with a foundational understanding of its decentralized and transparent nature. This sets the stage for comprehending its applications in agriculture. Exploring the benefits that Blockchain brings to agriculture, we highlight its capacity to enhance transparency, traceability, and overall efficiency within the supply chain. These insights lay the groundwork for envisioning a more accountable and resilient agricultural ecosystem. Real-world applications serve as compelling illustrations of Blockchain's transformative power. We delve into diverse use cases, demonstrating how Blockchain addresses specific challenges in agriculture, fostering trust and reliability.No technological revolution is without obstacles. Here, we candidly discuss the challenges hindering the widespread adoption of Blockchain in agriculture and propose practical solutions to facilitate its seamless integration. The exploration concludes with a reflection on the revolutionary potential of Blockchain in agriculture, urging stakeholders to embrace this transformative technology for a sustainable and efficient agricultural future.

Drones, once confined to the realms of aerial photography, have emerged as game-changers in agriculture. In this section, we embark on a historical journey of drones, unveiling their evolution and exploring their multifaceted role in modern farming practices. Tracing the origins of drones, we provide readers with a historical perspective, showcasing their transformation from military applications to indispensable tools in agriculture. Demystifying the technical aspects, we delve into the components and functioning of drones. This section empowers readers to understand the mechanics that make drones invaluable in agriculture. Highlighting the diverse applications, we showcase how drones contribute to various agricultural activities, from crop monitoring to precision farming. The emphasis is on increased productivity and resource optimization. Through real-world examples, we underscore the tangible benefits that drones bring to the agriculture sector, paving the way for increased efficiency and informed decision-making. Practical considerations play a crucial role. This section guides readers through key factors to consider, ensuring strategic and effective drone deployment in agriculture. Real-life scenarios exemplify the transformative impact of drones. Through compelling examples, we illustrate how drones address challenges and offer innovative solutions in agriculture. Identifying hurdles, this section addresses the challenges impeding the widespread adoption of drones in agriculture and proposes strategies for overcoming them. Looking ahead, we provide a futuristic perspective on how drones are poised to transform agriculture by 2025, offering insights into anticipated developments. The exploration concludes with a vision of drones as catalysts for a revolutionized agriculture sector, urging stakeholders to embrace this technological paradigm shift.

To foster critical engagement, this section presents thought-provoking assignment questions. These questions are designed to encourage readers to delve deeper into the content, promoting a thorough understanding of the subject matter. They serve as valuable tools for educators and self-learners alike.

As authors, we invite readers to immerse themselves in the exploration of these fundamental aspects of Agriculture Technology. Through the lenses of Blockchain, Drones, and the timeless principles of leadership from Kautilya's Arthashastra, we aspire to provide a holistic understanding that empowers individuals to navigate the dynamic intersection of technology and agriculture with confidence and foresight.

Authors

Contents

1

Role of Blockchain in Agriculture

Introduction

Blockchain technology has emerged as a revolutionary solution in various industries, and agriculture is no exception. By providing a secure and transparent system for recording and verifying transactions, blockchain has the potential to transform the agricultural sector. In this chapter, we will explore the role of blockchain in agriculture, its benefits, and various use cases that demonstrate its potential. Additionally, we will present key statistics and real-world examples to illustrate the impact of blockchain in agriculture.

1. Understanding Blockchain Technology

Before delving into the role of blockchain in agriculture, it is crucial to understand the fundamentals of blockchain technology. At its core, blockchain is a decentralized digital ledger that records and verifies transactions across multiple computers or nodes. The information stored in a blockchain is immutable and transparent, ensuring trust and eliminating the need for intermediaries.

Blockchain technology is a way of storing information in a way that makes it very difficult to change or hack. Blockchain is made up of blocks of data that are linked together in a chain. Each block contains a timestamp, a set of data, and a hash of the previous block. The hash is a unique identifier that is used to link the blocks together.

Blockchain technology can be used in a variety of ways in agriculture, including:

1. ***Food traceability:*** Blockchain can be used to track the movement of food products from farm to table. This can help to ensure food safety and traceability, and it can also help to prevent fraud.
2. ***Smart contracts:*** Blockchain can be used to create smart contracts, which are self-executing contracts that are stored on the blockchain. Smart contracts can be used to automate payments, track inventory, and manage supply chains.

3. ***Land registry:*** Blockchain can be used to create a secure and transparent land registry. This can help to prevent fraud and ensure that land ownership is accurately recorded.
4. ***Crop insurance:*** Blockchain can be used to create crop insurance policies that are more efficient and secure. This can help to protect farmers from financial losses in the event of crop failure.

Blockchain technology is still in its early stages of development, but it has the potential to revolutionize the agricultural industry. By making information more transparent and secure, blockchain can help to improve food safety, traceability, and efficiency. Here are some specific examples of how blockchain technology is being used in agriculture today:

1. ***IBM Food Trust:*** IBM Food Trust is a blockchain-based food traceability platform that is being used by a number of food companies, including Walmart, Dole, and Tyson Foods. The platform allows these companies to track the movement of food products from farm to table, ensuring food safety and traceability.
2. ***Provenance:*** Provenance is a blockchain-based platform that is being used by farmers and food producers to track the movement of food products. The platform allows these producers to share information about their products with consumers, ensuring transparency and trust.
3. ***CropIn:*** CropIn is a blockchain-based platform that is being used by farmers to manage their crops. The platform provides farmers with access to weather data, market information, and financial services. It also allows farmers to track the growth of their crops and to share this information with other farmers.

These are just a few examples of how blockchain technology is being used in agriculture today. As the technology continues to develop, we can expect to see even more innovative applications of blockchain in the agricultural industry.

2. Benefits of Blockchain in Agriculture

a. ***Improved food traceability:*** Blockchain can be used to track the movement of food products from farm to table, ensuring food safety and traceability.

b. ***Reduced food fraud:*** Blockchain can help to prevent food fraud by providing a secure and transparent way to track the movement of food products.

c. ***Increased efficiency:*** Blockchain can help to improve the efficiency of the agricultural supply chain by reducing paperwork and making transactions more secure.

d. ***Improved transparency:*** Blockchain can help to improve transparency in the agricultural industry by providing a way for all stakeholders to track the movement of food products.

e. ***Increased trust:*** Blockchain can help to increase trust between farmers, food producers, and consumers by providing a secure and transparent way to track the movement of food products.

f. ***Reduced costs:*** Blockchain can help to reduce costs in the agricultural industry by reducing paperwork and making transactions more efficient.

g. ***Improved decision-making:*** Blockchain can help farmers to make better decisions about their crops by providing them with access to real-time data about their crops and the market.

h. ***Increased access to finance:*** Blockchain can help farmers to access finance more easily by providing them with a way to track their crops and prove their ownership.

i. ***Improved land management:*** Blockchain can help to improve land management by providing a way to track land ownership and usage.

j. ***Reduced risk of pests and diseases:*** Blockchain can help to reduce the risk of pests and diseases by providing a way to track the movement of plants and animals.

k. ***Improved water management:*** Blockchain can help to improve water management by providing a way to track water usage and prevent water theft.

l. ***Increased resilience:*** Blockchain can help to increase the resilience of the agricultural industry by providing a way to track and respond to disruptions.

m. ***Improved compliance:*** Blockchain can help farmers to comply with regulations by providing a way to track their activities and prove their compliance.

n. ***Created new jobs:*** Blockchain has the potential to create new jobs in the agricultural industry, such as blockchain developers, blockchain consultants, and blockchain farmers.

o. ***Increased innovation:*** Blockchain can help to drive innovation in the agricultural industry by providing a platform for new applications and services.

p. ***Sustainability:*** Blockchain can help to make the agricultural industry more sustainable by providing a way to track and reduce emissions.

q. ***Transparency:*** Blockchain can help to increase transparency in the agricultural industry by providing a way for all stakeholders to track the movement of food products.

r. ***Security:*** Blockchain is a very secure technology, which can help to protect food products from fraud and contamination.

s. ***Scalability:*** Blockchain is a scalable technology, which means that it can be used to track a large number of food products.

t. ***Cost-effective:*** Blockchain is a cost-effective technology, which means that it can be used to track food products without incurring high costs.

3. Use Cases of Blockchain in Agriculture

Use Case 1: Supply Chain Traceability

a. ***Description:*** Blockchain can enable end-to-end traceability of agricultural products, ensuring transparency and authenticity. It allows tracking the journey of a product from farm to fork, providing consumers with detailed information about its origin, processing, and storage conditions.

b. ***Current Scenario:*** The lack of transparency in supply chains often leads to food fraud and safety concerns. Consumers are increasingly demanding more information about the products they consume.

c. ***How Blockchain Adds Value:*** Blockchain technology can securely record and store data about each step of the supply chain, including details about farming practices, transportation, and storage conditions. This transparency builds trust and ensures food safety.

d. ***Statistics:*** According to a survey conducted by Label Insight, 94% of consumers are likely to be loyal to a brand that offers transparency, including detailed information about product origin and quality.

e. ***Startups:*** Provenance, a UK-based startup, uses blockchain to trace the journey of seafood products, promoting sustainability and ethical sourcing.

Use Case 2: Certification and Quality Assurance

a. ***Description:*** Blockchain simplifies the certification process by securely storing and verifying data related to certifications and quality standards. This ensures that products meet the necessary requirements.

b. ***Current Scenario:*** Certification processes can be complex and prone to fraud. Consumers struggle to trust the authenticity and quality of agricultural products.

c. ***How Blockchain Adds Value:*** Blockchain provides a tamper-proof record of certifications and quality assurance, making it easier for consumers to verify the authenticity of products. This increases trust and helps maintain quality standards.

d. ***Statistics:*** A study by Label Insight found that 73% of consumers are willing to pay more for a product if it provides complete transparency, including information about certifications.

e. ***Startups:*** TE-Food, a blockchain-based platform, focuses on traceability and quality assurance for agricultural products, enabling transparency and trust in the supply chain.

Use Case 3: Land and Crop Management

a. ***Description:*** Blockchain streamlines land and crop management processes by securely recording and managing land titles, ownership, and crop data. It helps address issues related to land disputes, property rights, and agricultural financing.

b. ***Current Scenario:*** Land disputes and lack of secure ownership hinder agricultural development. Small-scale farmers often struggle to access financing due to insufficient collateral.

c. ***How Blockchain Adds Value:*** Blockchain-based land and crop management systems provide secure and immutable records of ownership, reducing disputes and enabling farmers to access credit and financial services.

d. ***Statistics:*** According to the World Bank, around 70% of land worldwide lacks proper documentation, leading to significant challenges for farmers, especially in developing countries.

e. ***Startups:*** Bitland, a Ghana-based startup, uses blockchain to digitize land records and provide secure land tenure systems, empowering farmers and improving land governance.

Use Case 4: Agricultural Insurance and Financing

a. ***Description:*** Blockchain technology can revolutionize agricultural insurance and financing by reducing fraud, improving risk assessment, and enhancing accessibility for small-scale farmers.

b. ***Current Scenario:*** Small-scale farmers often face challenges in obtaining insurance coverage and accessing credit due to limited financial resources and lack of proper documentation.

c. ***How Blockchain Adds Value:*** Blockchain-based systems automate the insurance claim settlement process and improve risk assessment. Smart contracts ensure prompt payouts, while transparent records enhance the creditworthiness of farmers.

d. ***Statistics:*** According to the International Finance Corporation, 90% of small-scale farmers in developing countries lack access to formal credit, resulting in an estimated $150 billion annual financing gap.

e. ***Startups:*** Etherisc, a blockchain-based insurance platform, offers parametric insurance for agriculture, reducing the cost and administrative burden associated with traditional insurance.

Use Case 5: Farmer Identity and Supply Chain Authentication

a. ***Description:*** Blockchain can securely store and verify farmer identities, ensuring that only genuine producers are part of the supply chain. It helps authenticate the origin of agricultural products.

b. ***Current Scenario:*** Counterfeit products and misrepresentation of farmer identities can damage trust in the supply chain. Consumers want assurance about the authenticity and ethical sourcing of products.

c. ***How Blockchain Adds Value:*** Blockchain-based identity management systems provide a reliable way to authenticate farmers and ensure their products are accurately represented. This enhances consumer trust and combats fraud.

d. ***Statistics:*** According to the Organization for Economic Cooperation and Development (OECD), counterfeit agricultural products account for approximately $30 billion annually.

e. ***Startups:*** AgUnity, an Australian startup, uses blockchain to create digital identities for farmers in developing countries, facilitating fairer trade and ensuring transparency in the supply chain.

Use Case 6: Farm-to-Consumer Direct Sales

a. ***Description:*** Blockchain enables direct sales between farmers and consumers, cutting out intermediaries and ensuring fairer prices for farmers while providing consumers with fresh and traceable products.

b. ***Current Scenario:*** Intermediaries in the agricultural supply chain often lead to higher prices for consumers and lower profits for farmers. Consumers are increasingly seeking local, fresh, and traceable products.

c. ***How Blockchain Adds Value:*** Blockchain-based platforms connect farmers directly with consumers, eliminating intermediaries and enabling transparent and fair transactions. Consumers can trace the product's journey, supporting local producers.

d. ***Statistics:*** The U.S. Department of Agriculture reports that the farmer's share of the food dollar is around 14.6 cents, with the rest going to processing, marketing, and distribution.

e. ***Startups:*** Ripe.io, a startup based in the United States, utilizes blockchain to connect farmers with consumers, enabling direct sales and ensuring transparency and freshness.

Use Case 7: Fair Trade and Ethical Sourcing

a. ***Description:*** Blockchain promotes fair trade and ethical sourcing by providing transparent and auditable records of transactions and certifications, ensuring that producers receive fair compensation.

b. ***Current Scenario:*** Lack of transparency and traceability in supply chains often results in exploitation of farmers and workers. Consumers are increasingly demanding ethically sourced products.

c. ***How Blockchain Adds Value:*** Blockchain creates an immutable and transparent record of transactions, certifications, and labor practices. This promotes fair trade, helps eliminate labor exploitation, and enables consumers to make informed choices.

d. ***Statistics:*** Fairtrade International reports that consumers spent over €11 billion ($12.8 billion) on Fairtrade-certified products in 2019.

e. ***Startups:*** Farmer Connect, a Swiss startup, uses blockchain to connect coffee farmers with consumers, promoting fair trade and enabling consumers to support ethical sourcing.

Use Case 8: Sustainable Agriculture and Carbon Footprint Tracking

a. ***Description:*** Blockchain can support sustainable agriculture by tracking and verifying sustainable farming practices and reducing the carbon footprint of agricultural products.

b. ***Current Scenario:*** Consumers are increasingly concerned about the environmental impact of agricultural practices. Proving sustainability claims can be challenging.

c. ***How Blockchain Adds Value:*** Blockchain provides a transparent and auditable platform to record and verify sustainable farming practices, carbon offset credits, and supply chain emissions. This fosters accountability and enables consumers to make environmentally conscious choices.

d. ***Statistics:*** The Food and Agriculture Organization estimates that the agriculture sector is responsible for approximately 14% of global greenhouse gas emissions.

e. ***Startups:*** Viant, an Ethereum-based platform, collaborates with various partners to track the carbon footprint of agricultural products and provide transparency in sustainable practices.

Use Case 9: Seed Provenance and Intellectual Property Protection

a. ***Description:*** Blockchain can ensure the provenance of seeds, protecting intellectual property rights of breeders and preserving biodiversity.

b. ***Current Scenario:*** Unauthorized seed reproduction and distribution impact the revenues of breeders and pose a risk to biodiversity conservation efforts.

c. ***How Blockchain Adds Value:*** Blockchain-based systems can securely record the origin and ownership of seeds, making it easier to protect intellectual property rights and maintain seed diversity.

d. ***Statistics:*** The International Treaty on Plant Genetic Resources for Food and Agriculture estimates that more than 90% of crop varieties have disappeared from farmers' fields, threatening global food security.

e. ***Startups:*** BlockGrain, an Australian startup, uses blockchain to trace and verify the origin of seeds, ensuring that breeders' intellectual property rights are protected.

Use Case 10: Farm Equipment Sharing and Rental

a. ***Description:*** Blockchain facilitates equipment sharing and rental platforms, enabling farmers to optimize equipment utilization, reduce costs, and foster collaboration.

b. ***Current Scenario:*** Owning and maintaining farm equipment can be expensive, especially for small-scale farmers. Equipment sharing platforms are often limited by trust and coordination challenges.

c. ***How Blockchain Adds Value:*** Blockchain-based platforms provide transparent and secure records of equipment ownership, rental agreements, and usage data. This builds trust and allows farmers to efficiently share and rent equipment.

d. ***Statistics:*** The U.S. Department of Agriculture estimates that the average annual ownership costs of farm machinery range from $1,700 for small tractors to $38,000 for large tractors.

e. ***Startups:*** WeFarmUp, a French startup, uses blockchain to create a decentralized platform for sharing and renting agricultural machinery, enabling cost savings and improved resource utilization.

Use Case 11: Marketplaces for Agricultural Products

a. ***Description:*** Blockchain-based marketplaces connect farmers with buyers, enabling efficient and transparent trade while reducing dependence on traditional intermediaries.

b. ***Current Scenario:*** Traditional agricultural marketplaces often involve numerous intermediaries and lack transparency, resulting in higher costs and limited market access for farmers.

c. ***How Blockchain Adds Value:*** Blockchain-based marketplaces provide direct connections between farmers and buyers, eliminating intermediaries and reducing transaction costs. The transparent nature of blockchain fosters trust and enables efficient trade.

d. ***Statistics:*** According to the World Bank, small-scale farmers in developing countries lose an estimated 60% of the value of their agricultural products due to inefficiencies in the supply chain.

e. ***Startups:*** GrainChain, a startup based in the United States, uses blockchain to create a marketplace for farmers and buyers, facilitating efficient and transparent trade while reducing transaction costs.

Use Case 12: Agricultural Data Management and Analysis

a. ***Description:*** Blockchain enables secure and decentralized data management, allowing farmers, researchers, and policymakers to access and contribute to a shared repository of agricultural data.

b. ***Current Scenario:*** Agricultural data is often fragmented and underutilized. Farmers, researchers, and policymakers face challenges in accessing and sharing relevant data for decision-making.

c. ***How Blockchain Adds Value:*** Blockchain-based data management platforms provide a secure and decentralized system for collecting, storing, and analyzing agricultural data. This promotes collaboration, innovation, and evidence-based decision-making.

d. ***Statistics:*** According to the World Economic Forum, the global agriculture industry generates vast amounts of data, with the potential to unlock $4.6 trillion of additional economic value annually.

e. ***Startups:*** AgriDigital, an Australian startup, uses blockchain to create a secure and transparent platform for managing agricultural data, enabling collaboration and data-driven insights for stakeholders.

Note: The startups mentioned in each use case are examples of companies operating in those specific areas and may not represent an exhaustive list. The landscape of startups in the blockchain and agriculture space is continuously evolving.

4. Challenges in Adoption of Blockchain in Agriculture and Solutions

Challenges in Adoption of Blockchain in Agriculture and Solutions are listed below. The initiatives mentioned by the Indian government are examples of efforts taken in the context of blockchain adoption in agriculture in India and may not represent an exhaustive list of initiatives.

1. Limited Technology Infrastructure

a. ***Challenge:*** In many rural areas, the lack of reliable internet connectivity and technological infrastructure hinders the adoption of blockchain in agriculture.

b. ***Solution:*** To address this challenge, improving internet connectivity and infrastructure in rural areas is crucial. Governments and organizations can invest in expanding broadband access and providing necessary hardware. Initiatives such as the BharatNet project in India aim to connect rural areas with high-speed internet, enabling the adoption of blockchain technology.

c. ***Initiatives by Indian Government:*** The Indian government's BharatNet project aims to connect over 250,000 village panchayats (local government institutions) with high-speed internet. This initiative helps create a conducive environment for the adoption of blockchain technology in rural areas.

d. ***Role of Academia:*** Academia can contribute by conducting research on low-bandwidth blockchain solutions, developing alternative connectivity options, and creating awareness among rural communities about the benefits of blockchain.

e. ***Startups:*** Startups can develop blockchain solutions that can function in low-connectivity environments and provide technical support to farmers in adopting blockchain technology.

2. Lack of Technical Skills and Awareness

a. ***Challenge:*** Farmers and other stakeholders in the agriculture sector may lack technical skills and awareness about blockchain technology, hindering its adoption.

b. ***Solution:*** Promoting technical education and awareness programs is crucial. Training programs, workshops, and capacity-building initiatives can be conducted to educate farmers, agricultural professionals, and policymakers about the potential of blockchain in agriculture. Collaborations between academia, industry, and government can facilitate these awareness initiatives.

c. ***Initiatives by Indian Government:*** The National Institute of Agricultural Extension Management (MANAGE) in India conducts training programs and workshops to educate agricultural professionals about emerging technologies, including blockchain.

d. ***Role of Academia:*** Academia can develop specialized courses and training programs on blockchain technology in agriculture. They can also conduct research to understand the specific challenges faced by farmers in adopting blockchain and develop user-friendly solutions.

e. ***Startups:*** Startups can contribute by organizing awareness campaigns, conducting training programs, and developing intuitive blockchain platforms tailored to the needs of farmers and other stakeholders.

3. Interoperability and Standardization

a. ***Challenge:*** The lack of interoperability and standardization across different blockchain platforms can create challenges in integrating and sharing data among stakeholders in the agricultural ecosystem.

b. ***Solution:*** Developing interoperable protocols and industry standards is essential to ensure seamless data sharing and integration. Efforts should be made to promote collaboration among blockchain platforms and establish common data formats and protocols. Consortia and industry alliances can play a significant role in driving interoperability initiatives.

c. ***Initiatives by Indian Government:*** The Indian government's National Blockchain Project aims to create a common infrastructure for different government departments, fostering interoperability and enabling secure and efficient data sharing.

d. ***Role of Academia:*** Academia can contribute by conducting research on interoperability standards, developing frameworks for data exchange, and collaborating with industry partners to establish common protocols.

e. ***Startups:*** Startups can develop interoperable blockchain solutions and participate in industry consortia to drive standardization efforts. They can also provide consultancy services to stakeholders seeking to integrate different blockchain platforms.

4. Privacy and Data Security

a. ***Challenge:*** Ensuring data privacy and security is a critical concern in blockchain adoption, as agricultural data often includes sensitive information such as farmer identities, land records, and financial transactions.

b. ***Solution:*** Implementing robust privacy and security measures is vital. Techniques such as encryption, digital signatures, and access controls can be employed to protect sensitive data. Compliance with data protection regulations and frameworks should be prioritized.

c. ***Initiatives by Indian Government:*** The Indian government has proposed the Personal Data Protection Bill, which aims to establish a framework for the protection and processing of personal data, safeguarding the privacy rights of individuals.

d. ***Role of Academia:*** Academia can conduct research on privacy-preserving technologies in blockchain, develop secure data storage and access mechanisms, and contribute to the formulation of data protection policies.

e. Startups: Startups can develop blockchain solutions with built-in privacy features, provide secure storage solutions, and assist farmers in implementing best practices for data privacy and security.

5. Scalability and Performance

a. ***Challenge:*** Blockchain technology faces scalability and performance limitations, especially when dealing with a large volume of transactions and data, which can be a challenge in the agricultural sector.

b. ***Solution:*** Innovations such as layer-two scaling solutions (e.g., sidechains, state channels), sharding, and off-chain data storage can help improve scalability and performance. Research and development efforts should focus on optimizing blockchain protocols and consensus algorithms for agricultural use cases.

c. ***Initiatives by Indian Government:*** The Indian government's Blockchain Technology Laboratory (BTL) initiative aims to develop scalable and sustainable blockchain solutions for various sectors, including agriculture.

d. ***Role of Academia:*** Academia can contribute by conducting research on scalability solutions, optimizing consensus algorithms, and developing efficient data storage and retrieval mechanisms.

e. ***Startups:*** Startups can develop scalable blockchain platforms and solutions that are tailored to the specific requirements of the agriculture sector. They can also collaborate with academia and industry to explore innovative approaches to scalability.

6. Cost of Implementation

a. ***Challenge:*** Implementing blockchain technology in agriculture can involve significant costs, including infrastructure setup, software development, and training.

b. ***Solution:*** Cost-effective implementation strategies should be explored. Leveraging cloud-based blockchain solutions, open-source platforms, and shared infrastructure can help reduce initial investment costs. Governments and organizations can provide financial incentives, grants, and subsidies to support blockchain adoption in agriculture.

c. ***Initiatives by Indian Government:*** The National e-Governance Division of India's Ministry of Electronics and Information Technology has launched the Blockchain-Based Secure Ecosystem for Farmers (BSF) initiative, which provides financial assistance and support to blockchain startups addressing agricultural challenges.

d. ***Role of Academia:*** Academia can collaborate with industry partners to develop cost-effective blockchain solutions, conduct cost-benefit analyses of blockchain adoption, and contribute to the formulation of government policies for funding and subsidies.

e. ***Startups:*** Startups can offer cost-effective blockchain solutions and services, participate in government-sponsored programs and initiatives, and leverage shared infrastructure to reduce implementation costs.

7. Regulatory and Legal Frameworks

a. ***Challenge:*** The absence of clear regulatory and legal frameworks specific to blockchain technology can create uncertainties and challenges in its adoption in agriculture.

b. ***Solution:*** Governments should proactively establish regulatory frameworks that address legal aspects such as data ownership, smart contracts, digital signatures, and dispute resolution. Engaging with industry stakeholders, legal experts, and policymakers is crucial to develop comprehensive and forward-looking regulations.

c. ***Initiatives by Indian Government:*** The Indian government's National Blockchain Strategy aims to develop a regulatory framework for blockchain technology, addressing legal and policy aspects.

d. ***Role of Academia:*** Academia can collaborate with legal experts and policymakers to conduct research on legal challenges related to blockchain adoption, provide inputs for regulatory frameworks, and educate stakeholders about legal implications.

e. ***Startups:*** Startups can actively engage with policymakers and industry associations to advocate for favorable regulatory frameworks and provide legal consulting services to stakeholders navigating blockchain adoption.

8. Resistance to Change and Adoption

a. ***Challenge:*** Resistance to change and lack of awareness among stakeholders can hinder the adoption of blockchain technology in the agricultural sector.

b. ***Solution:*** Creating awareness about the benefits of blockchain, its potential applications, and successful case studies is essential. Demonstrating the tangible value and positive impact of blockchain through pilot projects and proof-of-concept initiatives can help overcome resistance and encourage adoption.

c. ***Initiatives by Indian Government:*** The Indian Government's Atal Innovation Mission fosters innovation and entrepreneurship by supporting incubation centers and startup mentorship programs. Such initiatives can encourage blockchain startups to develop solutions for the agricultural sector.

d. ***Role of Academia:*** Academia can organize awareness campaigns, workshops, and training programs to educate stakeholders about blockchain technology, its benefits, and successful use cases. Collaborating with industry partners to conduct pilot projects can help demonstrate the value of blockchain in agriculture.

e. ***Startups:*** Startups can develop pilot projects and proof-of-concept initiatives in collaboration with farmers, agricultural cooperatives, and industry stakeholders to showcase the benefits of blockchain technology. They can also conduct awareness programs and provide training to facilitate adoption.

9. Integration with Existing Systems

a. ***Challenge:*** Integrating blockchain technology with existing agricultural systems, such as legacy databases and software, can be challenging due to compatibility issues and complex migration processes.

b. ***Solution:*** Integration strategies should be carefully planned and executed. Developing application programming interfaces (APIs) and middleware solutions can help bridge the gap between blockchain and existing systems. Collaborations between blockchain solution providers and existing software vendors can facilitate seamless integration.

c. ***Initiatives by Indian Government:*** The Indian government's National Blockchain Project aims to develop a common infrastructure that integrates blockchain with various government systems, enabling seamless data exchange and interoperability.

d. ***Role of Academia:*** Academia can research integration strategies and develop frameworks for seamless integration between blockchain and existing agricultural systems. They can collaborate with software vendors to identify compatibility challenges and develop solutions.

e. ***Startups:*** Startups can offer middleware solutions and APIs that facilitate integration between blockchain and existing agricultural systems. They can also collaborate with existing software vendors to develop interoperable solutions.

10. Environmental Impact

a. ***Challenge:*** The energy consumption associated with blockchain mining and validation processes can contribute to environmental concerns, including carbon emissions.

b. ***Solution:*** Exploring energy-efficient consensus algorithms, such as proof-of-stake, and leveraging renewable energy sources for blockchain operations can help mitigate the environmental impact. Improving the energy efficiency of blockchain protocols and promoting sustainable mining practices are crucial.

c. ***Initiatives by Indian Government:*** The Indian government has initiated the National Mission on Interdisciplinary Cyber-Physical Systems, which focuses on research and development of sustainable technologies, including blockchain.

d. ***Role of Academia:*** Academia can conduct research on energy-efficient consensus algorithms, develop frameworks for sustainable blockchain operations, and contribute to the adoption of renewable energy sources in blockchain infrastructure.

e. ***Startups:*** Startups can develop energy-efficient blockchain solutions, promote sustainable mining practices, and explore partnerships with renewable energy providers to reduce the environmental impact of blockchain operations.

Conclusion

Blockchain technology holds immense potential to revolutionize the agriculture industry. By providing transparency, traceability, and efficiency, blockchain can address various challenges and create new opportunities for farmers, distributors, and consumers. The use cases and statistics presented in this chapter highlight the significant impact of blockchain in agriculture and set the stage for a more sustainable, secure, and inclusive agricultural ecosystem. As the technology continues to evolve, further advancements and applications are expected to shape the future of agriculture.

2

Role of Drones in Agriculture Revolutionizing Farming Practices

Introduction

The use of drones, or Unmanned Aerial Vehicles (UAVs), in the agriculture sector has ushered in a new era of precision farming. These versatile flying machines equipped with advanced sensors and cameras have the potential to transform various agricultural activities, resulting in increased productivity, reduced costs, and more sustainable practices.

This chapter explores the history of drones, their components and functioning, the numerous agriculture activities where drones can be employed, the benefits they offer, real-world use cases, challenges in adoption, and possible solutions to fully realize their potential in the agriculture sector.

1. History of Drones

The history of drones traces back to the early 20th century, with the development of the first radio-controlled aircraft in the 1930s. However, it was during World War II that drones gained prominence for military reconnaissance and target practice. Post-war, drones found applications in research and surveillance, and by the 21st century, commercial and consumer drones emerged, including those tailored for agriculture.

2. Components and Functioning of Drones

Modern agricultural drones consist of several key components:

a. ***Frame:*** The drone's physical structure, usually made of lightweight materials for easy manoeuvrability.

b. ***Propellers and Motors:*** These provide the necessary lift and propulsion for the drone's flight.

c. ***GPS Module:*** Enables accurate positioning and navigation.

d. ***Sensors and Cameras:*** High-resolution cameras and various sensors (e.g., multispectral, thermal) capture essential data.

e. ***Onboard Computer:*** Processes data and controls flight parameters.

f. ***Communication Systems:*** Facilitate real-time data transmission between the drone and the operator.

Drones operate using a combination of GPS navigation, remote control, and autonomous flight modes. The GPS module ensures precise positioning, while the onboard computer, equipped with specialized software, interprets data from sensors and cameras, enabling the drone to carry out specific tasks.

3. Drones in Agriculture Activities

Drones find applications in various agriculture activities, including:

a. ***Crop Monitoring:*** Drones equipped with high-resolution cameras can capture detailed images of crops, helping farmers monitor growth patterns, detect pests, diseases, and nutrient deficiencies.

b. ***Precision Agriculture:*** By analysing data collected by drones, farmers can make informed decisions about precise irrigation, fertilization, and pesticide application, optimizing resource usage and maximizing yields.

c. ***Crop Spraying:*** Drones equipped with spraying systems deliver fertilizers, pesticides, or herbicides efficiently and accurately, minimizing waste and reducing human exposure to chemicals.

d. ***Planting:*** Drones can be programmed to plant seeds in predefined patterns, improving planting efficiency and promoting uniform crop growth.

e. ***Livestock Monitoring:*** Drones with thermal cameras aid in monitoring livestock health and behaviour, facilitating early disease detection and optimized livestock management.

4. Benefits of Drones in Agriculture Sector

Drones offer numerous advantages to farmers, including:

a. ***Enhanced Crop Health Monitoring:*** Drones provide real-time data, allowing early detection of potential crop issues, leading to timely interventions and increased yields.

b. ***Precision Farming:*** By precisely applying inputs like water, fertilizers, and pesticides, farmers can reduce costs, minimize environmental impacts, and increase overall farm efficiency.

c. ***Time and Labor Savings:*** Drones automate various tasks, saving farmers time and reducing the need for manual labour, especially in large agricultural fields.

d. ***Increased Safety:*** Drones minimize the exposure of farmers to hazardous substances during crop spraying, thus promoting safer agricultural practices.

e. ***Data-Driven Decision Making:*** The data collected by drones assists farmers in making informed decisions, optimizing their operations, and improving overall productivity.

There are several benefits to various stakeholders as articulated below.

1. Farmers

a. ***Improved crop monitoring:*** Drones can be used to monitor crops for pests, diseases, and other problems. This can help farmers to identify and address problems early, which can save them money and improve yields.

b. ***More efficient crop spraying:*** Drones can be used to spray crops with pesticides and fertilizers. This can be more efficient than traditional methods, and it can also help to reduce the risk of exposure to chemicals for farmers.

c. ***Improved yield forecasting:*** Drones can be used to collect data on crop health and growth. This data can be used to forecast yields, which can help farmers to make better decisions about planting, harvesting, and marketing.

d. ***Reduced labor costs:*** Drones can be used to perform tasks that would otherwise be done by hand, such as scouting crops, applying pesticides, and harvesting. This can save farmers money on labor costs.

2. Customers

a. ***Fresher produce:*** Drones can be used to deliver fresh produce directly to customers. This can reduce the time that produce spends in transit, which can improve its freshness.

b. ***More transparency:*** Drones can be used to provide customers with more transparency about the production of their food. This can include information about the farm where the food was grown, the methods used to grow it, and the people who produced it.

c. ***Better traceability:*** Drones can be used to track the movement of food from farm to table. This can help to ensure that food is safe and that it is not contaminated.

3. Investors

a. ***New investment opportunities:*** Drone technology is still in its early stages, which means that there are many new investment opportunities. Investors who get involved early could potentially see significant returns.

b. ***Improved risk assessment:*** Drones can be used to assess the risks associated with investments in agriculture. This can help investors to make better decisions about where to put their money.

c. ***Increased transparency:*** Drones can be used to provide investors with more transparency about the companies they are investing in. This can help investors to make better decisions about where to put their money.

4. Bulk buyers

a. ***More accurate inventory management:*** Drones can be used to track inventory levels in bulk warehouses. This can help buyers to ensure that they have enough product on hand to meet demand.

b. ***Improved quality control:*** Drones can be used to inspect bulk products for quality issues. This can help buyers to ensure that they are getting the best quality product possible.

c. ***Reduced transportation costs:*** Drones can be used to deliver bulk products directly to buyers. This can reduce transportation costs and improve the freshness of the product.

5. Factors to be considered while deploying drones in Agriculture sector

Some factors to consider while using drones in agriculture are listed below:

a. ***The type of drone:*** There are many different types of drones available, each with its own strengths and weaknesses. For example, some drones are better suited for crop monitoring, while others are better suited for crop spraying. It is important to choose the right drone for the specific task at hand.

b. ***The size of the farm:*** The size of the farm will also affect the type of drone that is needed. For example, a small farm may be able to get away with using a small, lightweight drone, while a large farm may need a larger, more powerful drone.

c. ***The climate:*** The climate in the area where the drone will be used is also an important factor to consider. For example, drones that are used in hot, dry climates will need to be able to withstand the heat and dust.

d. ***The regulations:*** It is important to be aware of the regulations that apply to drone use in the area where the drone will be used. For example, some countries require drones to be registered with the government.

e. ***The cost:*** The cost of drones can vary depending on the type of drone, the features it has, and the manufacturer. It is important to factor in the cost of the drone when making a business case for using drones in agriculture.

f. ***The potential benefits of using drones:*** Drones can offer a number of benefits for agriculture, such as improved crop monitoring, more efficient crop spraying, and reduced labor costs. It is important to quantify these benefits in order to make a strong business case for using drones.

g. ***The cost of using drones:*** The cost of using drones can include the cost of the drones themselves, the cost of training operators, and the cost of maintenance. It is important to factor in these costs when making a business case for using drones.

h. ***The risk of using drones:*** There are some risks associated with using drones, such as the risk of crashing the drone or the risk of violating regulations. It is important to assess these risks and to take steps to mitigate them.

Overall, using drones in agriculture can offer several benefits, but it is important to carefully consider the factors involved before making a business case for using drones.

6. Use Cases of Drones in Agriculture

1. Crop Health Monitoring

a. ***Description:*** Drones equipped with high-resolution cameras and multispectral sensors monitor crop health, identifying diseases, nutrient deficiencies, and stress.

b. ***Current Problem Scenario:*** Traditional crop monitoring methods are time-consuming and labour-intensive, leading to delayed detection of crop issues.

c. ***How Drones Add Value:*** Drones provide timely and accurate data on crop health, enabling farmers to take immediate action, reducing crop losses, and improving yields.

d. ***Statistics:*** According to a study by the American Society of Agronomy, drone-assisted crop monitoring can improve yields by up to 25%.

e. ***Challenges:*** High initial costs and the need for skilled operators to interpret data.

f. ***Solution:*** Government subsidies for drone adoption and training programs for farmers.

2. Precision Irrigation Management

a. ***Description:*** Drones equipped with sensors assess soil moisture levels, enabling precise irrigation planning.

b. ***Current Problem Scenario:*** Conventional irrigation practices often lead to overwatering or underwatering, resulting in water wastage or reduced yields.

c. ***How Drones Add Value:*** Drones optimize water usage by providing real-time soil moisture data, leading to water conservation and increased crop productivity.

d. ***Statistics:*** A study by the United Nations estimates that precision irrigation can reduce water usage by up to 40% while increasing crop yields by 20-30%.

e. ***Challenges:*** High-tech sensors require regular maintenance, and data analysis may require technical expertise.

f. ***Solution:*** Collaborations between drone manufacturers and agricultural experts to develop user-friendly sensors and data analysis software.

3. Crop Spraying

a. ***Description:*** Drones equipped with spraying systems deliver pesticides or fertilizers efficiently to specific areas of crops.

b. ***Current Problem Scenario:*** Manual spraying methods are time-consuming, imprecise, and can expose farmers to harmful chemicals.

c. ***How Drones Add Value:*** Drones offer precise application, reducing chemical wastage and minimizing human exposure to harmful substances.

d. ***Statistics:*** According to a study published in the International Journal of Agriculture and Biology, drone spraying can reduce pesticide usage by up to 30%.

e. ***Challenges:*** Regulatory restrictions on pesticide application via drones and limited payload capacity.

f. ***Solution:*** Collaboration between drone manufacturers, agricultural authorities, and environmental agencies to develop safe and compliant spraying protocols.

4. Planting

a. ***Description:*** Drones equipped with seed dispensers can plant seeds in pre-mapped patterns, ensuring uniformity and saving time and labour.

b. ***Current Problem Scenario:*** Manual planting can be labor-intensive, time-consuming, and lead to uneven crop growth.

c. ***How Drones Add Value:*** Drone planting improves planting efficiency, accelerates reforestation efforts, and ensures consistent crop density.

d. ***Statistics:*** BioCarbon Engineering's drone planting technology claims to achieve a planting rate of 120 trees per minute.

e. ***Challenges:*** Seed compatibility with the drone dispenser and accurate targeting of planting locations.

f. ***Solution:*** Collaboration between drone manufacturers and seed companies to develop drone-friendly seed technologies and advanced targeting algorithms.

5. Livestock Monitoring

a. ***Description:*** Drones equipped with thermal cameras and sensors monitor livestock health, behavior, and grazing patterns.

b. ***Current Problem Scenario:*** Traditional livestock monitoring methods may not cover large grazing areas, leading to delayed disease detection.

c. ***How Drones Add Value:*** Drones facilitate timely disease detection, enabling prompt veterinary intervention and improved livestock management.

d. ***Statistics:*** A study published in the Journal of Animal Science and Biotechnology reported that drone-assisted monitoring reduced disease mortality by 20%.

e. ***Challenges:*** Limited flight time and the need for automated flight paths to cover extensive grazing areas.

f. ***Solution:*** Integration of drone swarming technology to extend flight time and cover larger areas.

6. Soil Sampling

a. ***Description:*** Drones collect soil samples from various locations in the field for detailed analysis.

b. ***Current Problem Scenario:*** Manual soil sampling is labour-intensive, and sampling accuracy can be compromised.

c. ***How Drones Add Value:*** Drones provide efficient and accurate soil sampling, enabling farmers to make informed decisions on fertilization and soil amendments.

d. ***Statistics:*** A study published in the Journal of Sensors reported that drone-based soil sampling reduced sampling time by 80% compared to manual methods.

e. ***Challenges:*** Ensuring proper handling and labelling of collected soil samples during flight.

f. ***Solution:*** Development of automated soil sample collection systems with secure storage and labelling capabilities.

7. Weed Detection and Management

a. ***Description:*** Drones equipped with advanced imaging systems detect and map weed-infested areas in fields.

b. ***Current Problem Scenario:*** Manual weed scouting is time-consuming and often results in delayed or inadequate weed management.

c. ***How Drones Add Value:*** Drones provide real-time weed maps, allowing farmers to implement targeted and efficient weed control measures.

d. ***Statistics:*** A study conducted by the University of California, Davis, found that drone-based weed mapping reduced herbicide usage by 40%.

e. ***Challenges:*** Accurate weed species identification and integrating drone data with precision spraying systems.

f. ***Solution:*** Collaborations between agricultural researchers and drone manufacturers to develop AI-driven weed recognition software and precision spraying integration.

8. Pest Detection and Management

a. ***Description:*** Drones equipped with cameras and sensors identify pest infestations in crops.

b. ***Current Problem Scenario:*** Traditional pest scouting methods often miss early signs of infestations, leading to significant crop damage.

c. ***How Drones Add Value:*** Drones facilitate early detection of pests, enabling targeted pest management interventions and minimizing crop losses.

d. ***Statistics:*** A study by the Food and Agriculture Organization estimated that early pest detection through drones could save up to 50% of crop losses.

e. ***Challenges:*** Integration of automated pest recognition algorithms and real-time data transmission.

f. ***Solution:*** Collaboration between drone manufacturers and entomologists to develop AI-driven pest recognition algorithms and optimized communication systems.

9. Pollination Assistance

a. ***Description:*** Drones equipped with pollen dispensers assist in pollination for certain crops.

b. ***Current Problem Scenario:*** Declining bee populations and limited access to natural pollinators can hamper crop yields.

c. ***How Drones Add Value:*** Drones provide an alternative pollination method, ensuring consistent crop pollination and enhanced yields.

d. ***Statistics:*** A study by the University of Canterbury showed that drone pollination increased fruit set by up to 60% in certain crops.

e. ***Challenges:*** Developing effective pollen dispersal mechanisms and ensuring compatibility with crop species.

f. ***Solution:*** Research partnerships between drone manufacturers and crop scientists to optimize drone pollination techniques.

10. Flood Assessment and Damage Evaluation

a. ***Description:*** Drones survey flood-affected areas, providing real-time information on damage assessment and relief requirements.

b. ***Current Problem Scenario:*** Flood assessment using traditional methods is slow, limiting timely disaster response.

c. ***How Drones Add Value:*** Drones enable rapid and comprehensive flood assessment, aiding authorities in disaster management and resource allocation.

d. ***Statistics:*** In a study conducted by the University of California, drones reduced flood damage assessment time by 90% compared to manual methods.

e. ***Challenges:*** Ensuring drone operability in adverse weather conditions and real-time data analysis.

f. ***Solution:*** Development of ruggedized drones with weather-resistant features and real-time data processing capabilities.

11. Crop Insurance Assessment

a. ***Description:*** Drones capture high-resolution images of crop damage for accurate and efficient insurance assessment.

b. ***Current Problem Scenario:*** Manual assessment of crop damage for insurance claims is time-consuming and may lead to disputes.

c. ***How Drones Add Value:*** Drones provide clear visual evidence of crop damage, expediting insurance claim processing and minimizing fraud.

d. ***Statistics:*** A study by the International Journal of Remote Sensing reported that drone-assisted crop damage assessment reduced claim processing time by 50%.

e. ***Challenges:*** Standardizing drone data formats and integrating with insurance company workflows.

f. ***Solution:*** Collaboration between drone manufacturers, insurance companies, and regulatory authorities to establish standardized assessment protocols.

12. Land Surveying and Mapping

a. ***Description:*** Drones equipped with LiDAR or photogrammetry technology create high-precision maps of agricultural land.

b. ***Current Problem Scenario:*** Traditional land surveying methods are time-consuming and may lack accuracy.

c. ***How Drones Add Value:*** Drones provide fast and accurate land mapping, assisting in land management and decision-making.

d. ***Statistics:*** A study by the Journal of Applied Remote Sensing reported that drone-based land surveying reduced data collection time by up to 70%.

e. ***Challenges:*** Integrating drone mapping data with Geographic Information Systems (GIS) and ensuring data accuracy.

f. ***Solution:*** Collaboration between drone manufacturers and GIS experts to develop seamless data integration solutions.

13. Soil Erosion Monitoring

a. ***Description:*** Drones assess soil erosion patterns and identify vulnerable areas in agricultural fields.

b. ***Current Problem Scenario:*** Manual soil erosion monitoring is challenging and may miss critical erosion-prone spots.

c. ***How Drones Add Value:*** Drones provide comprehensive and timely soil erosion data, aiding in erosion control and conservation efforts.

d. ***Statistics:*** According to the Journal of Hydrology, drone-based soil erosion monitoring reduced data collection time by 80% compared to conventional methods.

e. ***Challenges:*** Developing erosion detection algorithms and automating drone flight paths.

f. ***Solution:*** Collaborations between drone manufacturers, environmental scientists, and soil conservation experts to develop advanced erosion detection algorithms and automated flight planning systems.

14. Nutrient Mapping and Variable Rate Application

a. ***Description:*** Drones equipped with sensors assess soil nutrient levels and facilitate variable rate nutrient application.

b. ***Current Problem Scenario:*** Uniform nutrient application may lead to over or under-fertilization, impacting crop yields.

c. ***How Drones Add Value:*** Drones enable site-specific nutrient application, optimizing fertilizer usage, and enhancing crop nutrient uptake.

d. ***Statistics:*** A study by the American Society of Agronomy reported that drone-based variable rate nutrient application increased crop yields by up to 15%.

e. ***Challenges:*** Integrating drone data with variable rate application systems and ensuring accurate nutrient mapping.

f. ***Solution:*** Collaboration between drone manufacturers, agronomists, and agricultural equipment companies to develop seamless integration between drones and variable rate applicators.

15. Agricultural Inventory Management

a. ***Description:*** Drones equipped with RFID technology or barcode scanners track and manage agricultural inventory.

b. ***Current Problem Scenario:*** Manual inventory management can be error-prone and time-consuming.

c. ***How Drones Add Value:*** Drones streamline inventory tracking, reducing manual efforts and improving supply chain efficiency.

d. ***Statistics:*** A study by the Journal of Manufacturing Systems reported that drone-assisted inventory management reduced processing time by up to 60%.

e. ***Challenges:*** Ensuring compatibility with existing inventory management systems and tracking accuracy.

f. ***Solution:*** Collaboration between drone manufacturers and inventory management software developers to develop user-friendly integration solutions.

16. Drought Monitoring

a. ***Description:*** Drones equipped with thermal sensors and moisture detectors monitor drought-affected regions.

b. ***Current Problem Scenario:*** Traditional drought monitoring methods may lack real-time data and comprehensive coverage.

c. ***How Drones Add Value:*** Drones offer real-time drought monitoring, enabling timely intervention and resource allocation.

d. ***Statistics:*** A study by the United Nations estimated that drone-based drought monitoring reduced response time by up to 70%.

e. ***Challenges:*** Developing automated drought detection algorithms and ensuring consistent drone operability during drought conditions.

f. ***Solution:*** Collaborations between drone manufacturers, meteorologists, and drought response agencies to develop AI-driven drought detection algorithms and robust drone systems.

17. Agroforestry Planning

a. ***Description:*** Drones equipped with LiDAR technology assist in agroforestry planning and plantation layout.

b. ***Current Problem Scenario:*** Manual planning of agroforestry may lead to inefficient resource utilization and reduced benefits.

c. ***How Drones Add Value:*** Drones provide 3D mapping data, aiding in precise agroforestry planning and optimal resource allocation.

d. ***Statistics:*** A study by the Journal of Applied Remote Sensing reported that drone-based agroforestry planning reduced resource allocation errors by up to 90%.

e. ***Challenges:*** Integrating drone mapping data with agroforestry planning software and ensuring accurate tree positioning.

f. ***Solution:*** Collaboration between drone manufacturers, agroforestry experts, and software developers to develop user-friendly planning tools and seamless data integration.

18. Yield Estimation

a. ***Description:*** Drones equipped with remote sensing technology estimate crop yields across agricultural fields.

b. ***Current Problem Scenario:*** Manual yield estimation can be time-consuming and may lack accuracy.

c. ***How Drones Add Value:*** Drones provide rapid and accurate yield estimates, assisting farmers in crop marketing and post-harvest planning.

d. ***Statistics:*** A study published in the Journal of Imaging Science and Technology reported that drone-based yield estimation reduced estimation time by up to 80%.

e. ***Challenges:*** Developing precise yield estimation algorithms and automating data analysis.

f. ***Solution:*** Collaborations between drone manufacturers, agronomists, and agricultural economists to develop advanced yield estimation algorithms and user-friendly analysis tools.

19. Post-Harvest Inspection

a. ***Description:*** Drones equipped with cameras and sensors inspect post-harvest storage facilities for quality control.

b. ***Current Problem Scenario:*** Manual inspection of storage facilities can be labor-intensive and may miss potential issues.

c. ***How Drones Add Value:*** Drones provide comprehensive post-harvest inspections, facilitating early detection of quality issues and reducing post-harvest losses.

d. ***Statistics:*** A study by the International Journal of Agricultural and Biological Engineering reported that drone-assisted post-harvest inspection reduced inspection time by up to 70%.

e. ***Challenges:*** Developing automated inspection algorithms and integrating drone data with quality control systems.

f. ***Solution:*** Collaboration between drone manufacturers, quality control experts, and post-harvest management companies to develop AI-driven inspection algorithms and data integration protocols.

20. Land Use Planning

a. ***Description:*** Drones equipped with GIS technology create detailed land-use maps for agricultural planning.

b. ***Current Problem Scenario:*** Manual land-use planning can be time-consuming and may lack precision.

c. ***How Drones Add Value:*** Drones provide high-precision land-use maps, assisting farmers in efficient land management and decision-making.

d. ***Statistics:*** A study by the Journal of Applied Remote Sensing reported that drone-based land-use mapping reduced planning time by up to 60%.

e. ***Challenges:*** Integrating drone mapping data with land-use planning software and ensuring accuracy in land classification.

f. ***Solution:*** Collaboration between drone manufacturers, GIS experts, and agricultural land planners to develop seamless data integration and accurate classification techniques.

21. Farm Infrastructure Inspection

a. ***Description:*** Drones equipped with cameras and sensors inspect farm infrastructure, such as irrigation systems and buildings.

b. ***Current Problem Scenario:*** Manual infrastructure inspection can be challenging and may lead to delayed maintenance.

c. ***How Drones Add Value:*** Drones provide efficient and comprehensive infrastructure inspection, facilitating timely maintenance and reducing downtime.

d. ***Statistics:*** A study published in the Journal of Field Robotics reported that drone-assisted infrastructure inspection reduced inspection time by up to 75%.

e. ***Challenges:*** Developing automated inspection algorithms for different types of farm infrastructure and ensuring drone navigational safety.

f. ***Solution:*** Collaboration between drone manufacturers, agricultural engineers, and maintenance experts to develop specialized inspection algorithms and safe navigational protocols.

22. Agricultural Education and Extension

a. ***Description:*** Drones equipped with cameras and sensors assist agricultural extension officers in demonstrating best practices to farmers.

b. ***Current Problem Scenario:*** Conventional agricultural extension methods may lack visual demonstrations, limiting understanding.

c. ***How Drones Add Value:*** Drones provide visual demonstrations of agricultural techniques, enhancing farmer education and adoption of best practices.

d. ***Statistics:*** A study published in the Journal of Extension Education reported that drone-assisted agricultural extension increased adoption rates of recommended practices by up to 40%.

e. ***Challenges:*** Ensuring drone operability in various agricultural settings and developing interactive education content.

f. ***Solution:*** Collaboration between drone manufacturers, agricultural extension services, and education specialists to develop user-friendly drone systems and engaging educational content.

The use of drones in the agriculture sector has opened up a plethora of opportunities for farmers to enhance productivity, optimize resource usage, and improve overall efficiency. From crop health monitoring to agricultural education, drones are transforming various aspects of farming practices.

7. Challenges in Adoption of Drones in Agriculture Sector

1. Challenge: High Initial Investment

a. ***Solution:*** Government subsidies and financial assistance programs can be introduced to incentivize farmers to adopt drone technology. Additionally, academia and researchers can collaborate with drone manufacturers to develop affordable and cost-effective drone solutions tailored to the needs of small-scale farmers.

b. Contribution

- Government: Implement subsidy programs and financial incentives.
- Academia and Researchers: Conduct studies to identify cost-effective drone technologies.
- Industry and Startups: Develop budget-friendly drone models suitable for agricultural applications.

2. Challenge: Regulatory Restrictions

a. ***Solution:*** Collaboration between industry stakeholders, academia, and government bodies can lead to the development of comprehensive and farmer-friendly drone regulations. Awareness programs and training initiatives can be organized to educate farmers about these regulations and ensure responsible drone use.

b. Contribution:

- Government: Work with industry experts to formulate drone-friendly regulations.
- Academia and Researchers: Conduct studies on the impact of drones in agriculture to inform policy decisions.
- Industry and Startups: Participate in regulatory discussions and develop educational materials for farmers.

3. Challenge: Lack of Skilled Operators

a. ***Solution:*** Training programs conducted by academia, cooperatives, and industry players can be introduced to provide farmers with the necessary skills to operate drones and interpret data effectively.

b. Contribution:

- Academia and Researchers: Develop comprehensive training modules for drone operation and data analysis.
- Cooperatives and Industry: Organize training workshops and sessions for farmers.
- Government: Fund skill development programs for farmers.

4. Challenge: Data Management and Analysis

a. Solution: Collaborations between academia, researchers, and industry can lead to the development of user-friendly data analysis software, making it easier for farmers to interpret drone-collected data.

b. Contribution:

- Academia and Researchers: Develop data analysis algorithms and software tailored to agricultural needs.
- Industry: Create user-friendly data analysis platforms.
- Farmers and Cooperatives: Adopt and use data analysis tools for informed decision-making.

5. Challenge: Limited Flight Time

a. Solution: Industry and researchers can focus on developing drone technologies with extended flight times and efficient battery management systems.

b. Contribution:

- Industry and Startups: Invest in research and development to improve drone battery life.
- Researchers: Conduct studies on battery technology advancements for drone applications.

6. Challenge: Integration with Existing Farming Practices

a. Solution: Farmers, cooperatives, and industry players can work together to identify specific farming tasks where drones can add value and seamlessly integrate them into existing workflows.

b. Contribution:

- Farmers and Cooperatives: Identify areas where drones can enhance efficiency and productivity.
- Industry: Develop customized drone solutions to meet specific agricultural needs.

7. Challenge: Data Security and Privacy

a. Solution: Collaborations between industry and government can lead to the development of robust data security measures, ensuring that sensitive farm data collected by drones is protected.

b. Contribution:

- Industry: Implement encryption and secure data storage solutions.
- Government: Develop data protection guidelines and regulations.

8. Challenge: Adverse Weather Conditions

a. Solution: Researchers and industry players can work together to develop weather-resistant drones capable of operating under adverse weather conditions.

b. Contribution:

- Researchers: Conduct studies on drone resilience in extreme weather conditions.
- Industry: Design ruggedized drones suitable for agricultural environments.

9. Challenge: Compatibility with Existing Agricultural Equipment

a. Solution: Researchers and industry can collaborate to develop drone technologies that are compatible with existing agricultural machinery and equipment.

b. Contribution:

- Researchers: Study equipment integration possibilities and develop standardized protocols.
- Industry and Startups: Design drones with adaptability to existing equipment.

10. Challenge: Accessibility to Remote Areas

a. Solution: Government support and investment can help improve infrastructure in remote agricultural areas, enabling farmers to access and benefit from drone technology.

b. Contribution:

- Government: Fund infrastructure development projects in rural and remote areas.
- Industry: Develop lightweight and portable drones suitable for remote operation.

11. Challenge: Reliability and Maintenance

a. Solution: Industry and researchers can focus on designing robust and easily maintainable drone systems, and farmers can undergo training on drone maintenance and troubleshooting.

b. Contribution:

- Industry: Develop drones with durable components and easy maintenance features.

- Researchers: Conduct studies on drone reliability and maintenance best practices.
- Farmers: Undergo training in drone maintenance and troubleshooting.

12. Challenge: Limited Awareness and Acceptance

a. Solution: Awareness campaigns led by government, cooperatives, and industry can educate farmers about the benefits of drone technology in agriculture.

b. Contribution:

- Government: Organize awareness programs & disseminate information about drone adoption.
- Cooperatives: Educate their members about the advantages of using drones in farming.
- Industry: Participate in farmer outreach programs to showcase the value of drone technology.

By collectively addressing these challenges and fostering collaboration among academia, researchers, industry players, startups, farmers, cooperatives, and government entities, the adoption of drone technology in the agriculture sector can be accelerated, leading to increased productivity, sustainability, and overall progress in farming practices.

8. How would drones transform agriculture sector by 2025?

By 2025, drones are expected to have a transformative impact on the agriculture sector, revolutionizing traditional farming practices and contributing to sustainable and efficient agricultural operations. There are several ways drones are likely to transform the agriculture sector by 2025:

1. ***Precision Farming:*** Drones equipped with advanced sensors and imaging technology will enable precision farming practices. Farmers will be able to analyse real-time data on crop health, nutrient levels, and water requirements, leading to optimized resource allocation and increased crop yields.
2. ***Automated Operations:*** Drones will play a significant role in automating various agricultural tasks, such as planting, spraying, and monitoring. This will reduce the need for manual labour, saving time and costs for farmers.
3. ***Increased Efficiency:*** Drones will allow farmers to cover large agricultural areas quickly and efficiently, leading to faster data collection and decision-making. This increased efficiency will result in better farm management and productivity.

4. ***Environmental Sustainability:*** Drones will help farmers adopt more sustainable agricultural practices by enabling targeted application of fertilizers and pesticides, reducing chemical wastage, and minimizing environmental impacts.

5. ***Crop Monitoring and Disease Detection:*** Drones equipped with high-resolution cameras and multispectral sensors will facilitate early detection of diseases, pests, and nutrient deficiencies in crops. This proactive approach will help farmers take timely corrective measures, reducing crop losses.

6. ***Water Management:*** Drones will assist in precise irrigation management by monitoring soil moisture levels and crop water requirements. This will lead to optimized water usage, conserving water resources and ensuring better crop health.

7. ***Livestock Management:*** Drones equipped with thermal cameras will aid in livestock monitoring, enabling farmers to detect health issues, monitor grazing patterns, and improve overall livestock management.

8. ***Soil Health Assessment:*** Drones will play a crucial role in assessing soil health and fertility. By collecting soil samples and analysing data, farmers will be able to make informed decisions about soil management and amendments.

9. ***Rapid Response to Natural Disasters:*** In the event of natural disasters such as floods or wildfires, drones will be instrumental in conducting rapid assessments of damage, facilitating quicker response and relief efforts.

10. ***Data-Driven Decision Making:*** Drones will generate vast amounts of data on crop health, weather patterns, and soil conditions. Analysing this data will enable farmers to make data-driven decisions, improving overall farm efficiency.

11. ***Access to Remote Areas:*** Drones will provide access to remote and challenging terrains, allowing farmers in isolated regions to benefit from modern agricultural technologies and practices.

12. ***Education and Extension:*** Drones will be used to disseminate agricultural knowledge and best practices through visual demonstrations, empowering farmers with the latest information and techniques.

13. ***Integration with Smart Farming Technologies:*** Drones will seamlessly integrate with other smart farming technologies, such as Internet of Things (IoT) devices, artificial intelligence, and data analytics, creating a cohesive and interconnected agricultural ecosystem.

14. ***Real-Time Crop Mapping:*** Drones will generate high-resolution maps of agricultural fields, helping farmers identify areas with varying crop health and enabling site-specific interventions.
15. ***Crop Breeding and Research:*** Drones will facilitate research and development in crop breeding by providing detailed data on plant traits and growth patterns.

Overall, integration of drones into the agriculture sector by 2025 will enhance productivity, sustainability, and profitability for farmers, while also contributing to food security and environmental conservation on a global scale. As technology continues to advance, drones will become increasingly accessible and tailored to specific agricultural needs, leading to significant advancements in the way farming is practiced and managed.

Conclusion

Drones have emerged as powerful tools in revolutionizing agriculture by enabling precision farming, enhancing crop health monitoring, and optimizing resource usage. The integration of drone technology in agriculture has the potential to address the challenges posed by global food security and environmental sustainability. As drone technology continues to advance and costs decrease, more farmers can benefit from these transformative devices.

Assignment Questions

1. Explain the historical evolution of drones and their applications in the agriculture sector.
2. Describe the key components of agricultural drones and their functioning.
3. List and elaborate on five agriculture activities where drones can assist farmers, providing examples of real-world use cases.
4. Discuss the benefits of using drones in the agriculture sector, including their impact on crop health, resource management, and labour savings.
5. Choose two use cases of drones in agriculture and provide statistics and examples of startups that are implementing these solutions.
6. Identify and discuss the main challenges hindering the widespread adoption of drones in the agriculture sector.
7. Propose potential solutions to address the challenges and promote the adoption of drone technology in agriculture.
8. How would drones transform Agriculture sector by 2025? Elaborate 10 points.

3

Principles of Leadership from Kautilya's Arthashastra (Chanakya's Saptang Model)

Kautilya or Chanakya - probably the world's first Management Guru who was well known for his management models and strategies - is not the first strategist or author to write the *Arthashastra*. There were lot of gurus - *purva acharya*s - and leaders before him. Chanakya studied them all and compiled them into one book known as *Kautilya's Arthashastra*. The book was written centuries ago when the country was ruled by kings. But Chanakya had so much wisdom and foresight that, each time you read it, you will discover something new, something different.

The world has changed so much since he wrote the book. We are in the digital age now. But the basic principles haven't changed. They are eternal. Even almost 2300 years later, we all want the same thing - we want to live a healthy life, a life that has quality. And Chanakya tells you exactly how to do that.

Across the globe, leadership is a subject of serious discussion, study, and research. Universities now have centers of leadership. Many times, in an organization, the members become specialized in their particular field and department but they miss out on the complete picture. The leadership ideas of Chanakya give an insight into some strategic sutras which are simple and easy to understand yet powerful and impactful when applied. Chanakya's futuristic and time tested sutras relating to Philosophy and Ethics, Thought leadership, Qualities of a leader and Power and Responsibility, etc. will be explored in this chapter.

Who Was Chanakya?

- Born in the 4th Century BC in India, Chanakya was also known as Vishnugupta and Kautilya!
- Chanakya: A rare Mastermind who became an expert in varied and specialized field like ….

• Management • Economics • Politics • Law • Leadership • Governance • Warfare	• Military Tactics • Strategy • Finance • Accounting & • Several others like Astrology, Astronomy, Metallurgy, Medicine, etc.

- He was responsible for bringing down the Nanda dynasty and establishing his able student, Chandragupta Maurya on the throne as the Emperor, hence called the "King Maker"
- Chanakya mastermind the defeat of Alexander in India (who was on the march to conquer the world)
- Chanakya visualized the Concept of "Nation" for the first time in Human History, as during his time India was split into various Kingdoms
- He brought them all together under one central governance
- Thus creating a nation called Aryavartha, later became India
- Chanakya documented his lifelong work in his books:
    - Kautilya's Arthashastra
    - Chanakya Niti
- Kautilya's Arthashastra (KA) has 6000 Sutras, classified into 15 books, 150 Chapters and 180 Topics by Chanakya himself
- Many philosophical concepts about Leadership in KA like …
    - Aanvikshiki (The Science of Thinking)
    - Rajrishi (Philosopher King)
    - Indriyajaya (One who has control over himself)
    - Vijigishu (Conqueror)

    …… are India's unique contributions to the world
- For ages, rulers across the world have referred to the Arthashastra for building a nation on sound economics, based on spiritual value

The Process of Writing the Arthashastra

- Arthashastra literal translation: "Scripture of Wealth" but
- It's Knowledge of Wealth and a Wealth of Knowledge!
- Chanakya in opening sutra of KA starts by writing ….

"This single treatise on the science of politics has been prepared mostly by bringing together the teaching of as many treatises on the science of

politics as have been composed by ancient teachers for the acquisition and protection of the earth"….(KA: 1.1.1)

- Chanakya openly declares that his work is a collection of many works

The Purpose of Writing the Arthashastra

- Kautilya had written Arthashastra – for the Acquisition and Protection of Earth
- KA was written primarily for leaders, the Kings of his generation, and specially for Chandragupta Maurya …

"This science has been composed by him (Kautilya), who in resentment quickly regenerated the science and the weapons and the earth that was under the control of Nanda kings." …. (KA 15.1.73)

- Chanakya referring himself (above), that he in anger and frustration had dethroned the last King of the Nanda Dynasty (Dhanananda) and regenerated – meaning, recreated - the whole Art of Good Governance (The Science of Politics) through this work, The Arthashastra
- Chanakya concludes the Arthashastra by once again asserting the purpose of his writing…

"Seeing the manifold errors of the writers of commentaries on scientific treatises, Vishnugupta himself composed the sutras as well as the bhasya ." …. (KA End Note)

- It is responsibility of every generation to correct errors in the past writings. You cannot change the works of the past, but you can avoid making same errors in future works
- Salutations to this great master who learnt from the other masters. He teaches us never to condemn those before us, but to improve upon their teachings

How to Think?

- During every stage of life – as a child, student, teenager, professional, homemaker – you are constantly advised by others to "THINK" – to Avoid Mistakes and Succeed in Life
- But has any one actually taught you – "How to Think?"
- No for the first time – You are Thinking about Thinking
- Good news is that – Thinking can be taught!
- Chanakya was different personality – he said something he meant it. What he achieved in his life was due to a well-thought-out plan

- This process of Thinking is called AANVIKSHIKI
- Read Kautilya's Arthashastra in detail at some point in life as it can change your thinking – It teaches you how to think – like a Leader

Introduction to Aanvikashiki

Aanvikshiki

- Welcome to this New Word
- Welcome to a New Science
- Welcome to a New Subject
- Welcome to a New Way of Thinking
- Welcome to a completely New World Altogether

Aanvikashiki in Kautilya's Aarthashastra

- KA: First chapter talks about Aanvikshiki and its importance
- The Prathama Prakarna (First Section), named "Vidyasamuddesha" (Enumeration of the Sciences), starts with the Chapter "Aanvikshiki Sthapana" (Establishing the necessity of Thinking)
- Chanakya wants his students to study Aanvikshiki as their first subject – What an amazing way to begin
- Imagine teaching "Thinking" as 1st subject in our education system – We need to move into process of investigation and inquiry
- Let us teach our children to think & wonder, to imagine, to construct, to create, to dream, to visualize and to build their own future in a unique manner
- Chanakya wanted his students to be Leaders and first Quality of Leadership is to Think Correctly & Clearly

KA: Book 1, Section 1: "Aanvikshiki Sthapana":

- Right Thinking (Aanvikshiki), the Three Vedas (Trai), Economics (Varta) and the Science of Politics (Dandaniti) – these are the Sciences (Vidya)
- According to Kautilya, all four indeed are necessary sciences, since with their help one can learn what is spiritually good and material well-being
- Sankhya, Yoga & Lokayata: these constitute Aanvikshiki
- Investigating by means of reasoning, what is spiritual good and evil in the Vedic lore, material gain and loss in economics, good policy and bad policy

in the science of politics, as well as the relative strength and weakness of these sciences, Aanvikshiki confers benefits on the people, keeps the mind steady in adversity and prosperity and brings about proficiency in though, speech and action

- Aanvikshiki is always thought of as the lamp of all sciences, as the means of all actions and as the support of all laws and duties.

Dr. R.P. Kangle (A Sanskrit teacher at the University of Mumbai), who translated the original Sanskrit Kautilya's Arthashastra in English - refers to **Aanvikshiki as a philosophy** in his English translation

Aanvikashiki

"Right Thinking (Aanvikshiki), the Three Vedas (Trai), Economics (Varta) and the Science of Politics (Dandaniti) – these are the Sciences (Vidya)."

- As per Kautilya - There are four Vidyas (subjects) that student has to learn
- These 4 types of knowledge are fundamental to become Good Leader

1. Aanvikshiki: The Science of Thinking (Philosophical Thinking)
2. Trai: the 3 Vedas (Rig, Sama, Yajur) in the later generations. Atharva Veda was added as 4th Veda
3. Varta: Economics (Agriculture, Cattle-rearing and Trade): These were 3 primary economic activities during that time
4. Dandaniti: Political Science (The science of punishment and good governance)

- According to Chanakya, all the 4 Vidyas are important, yet, Aanvikshiki, the Right way of Thinking, should be given its due place in the field of knowledge
- One cannot just be materially rich and spiritually poor and vice versa
- Indian wisdom teaches us to both spiritually and materially developed

Aanvikashiki: It is a philosophy, which includes 3 other philosophies:

- Sankhya: One of the oldest philosophies by Kapila Muni.

  It is mentioned in second chapter of Bhagavat Gita

  Comes from word Samkhya, meaning 'Numbers"
- Yoga: Popular method of exercise to keep physical fitness

  But Yoga besides physical level, also keeps you fit at the level of mind, the intellectual and spiritual level

Sage Patanjali wrote Yoga sutras (Ashtanga Style)

Yoga comes from the root word yuj which means "to join or connect"

- Lokayata: This is another school of thought (Charvaka)

  Often referred to as Materialistic Philosophy

  In our culture, even materialistic thought is also respected

- Hence we can interpret Aanvikshiki as a way of thinking
  - Which includes Numbers (Sankya)
  - The right connection to divine (Yoga)
  - Material success (Lokayata)
- A person who thinks simultaneously in numbers, divine connections as well as material success is one who practice Aanvikshiki – A very Practical way of Thinking

How to Practice Aanvikashiki

"Investigating by means of reasoning, what is spiritual good and evil in the Vedic lore, material gain and loss in economics, good policy and bad policy in the science of politics, as well as the relative strength and weakness of these sciences."

- One needs to investigate with reason (Logically & systematically)
- Practicing Aanvikshiki requires to consider 3 things:
  1. Good & Evil (according to Vedic Tradition / Trai)
  2. Material Gain or Loss (According to Economics / Varta)
  3. Good Policy & Bad Policy (According to Science of Politics / Dandaniti)
- Thus, when we consider various dimensions, we will be able to take the right & correct decision, weighing all consequences

What are the Benefit of Aanvikshiki

"Aanvikshiki confers benefits on the people, keeps the mind steady in adversity and prosperity and brings about proficiency in though, speech and action".

- Aanvikshiki keeps mind steady in all situations
- It keeps ourselves calm and composed
- Practice of Aanvikashiki helps maintain the balance of mind

- It brings about proficiency in
    1. Though – it gives clear thinking (clairvoyance)
    2. Speech – verbal communication
    3. Action – there is perfection in all activities

"Aanvikshiki is always thought of as the lamp of all sciences, as the means of all actions and as the support of all laws and duties."

- This is the ultimate praise Chanakya accords to Aanvikshiki
- It is like a lamp guiding us in darkness
- Guiding lamp (Pradeep) of all sciences – it is the means and method of taking the right action : supporter of all laws and duties
- Whatever we do using Aanvikshiki as our foundation will be perfectly planned and executed and results are guaranteed
- And all this will be ethical, legal, moral & spiritual
- It will be completely Dharmic, abiding laws and duties

Types of Thinking

- Chanakya gives us indication of various types of thinking he practiced and preached
- You don't have to choose one and stick to it
- Different types of thinking can be used together
- Types of Thinking are as follows ....
    1. Both-side Thinking
    2. Alternative Thinking
    3. Leadership Thinking
    4. Creative Thinking
    5. Lateral Thinking
    6. Spiritual Thinking

Ideal Leadership Model - Rajarishi

- Rajarishi is combination of two words, "Raja" & "Rishi"
- Raja means a king or leader, Rishi means a sage / thinker
- For Chanakya ideal ruler is like a "Philosopher King"

In KA Book 1, Chapter 7, Sutra 1 Chanakya describe *Rajarishi* as

"By casting the group of six enemies, he should acquire control over the senses, cultivate his intellect by association with elders, keep a watchful

eye by means of spies, being about security and well-being by (energetic) activity, maintain the observances of their special duties (by the subjects) by carrying out his own duties, acquire discipline by receiving instruction in the sciences (different fields of knowledge), attain popularity by association with what is of material advantage and maintain proper behavior by doing what is beneficial."

By casting out the group of six enemies

- There are enemies outside and inside a kingdom
- Internal enemies are more dangerous than the external
- If one manages the internal enemies, it would be easy to control the external enemies
- Our primary internal enemies are: Lust, Anger, Greed, Pride, Arrogance and Foolhardiness
    - Lust: Over indulgence
    - Anger: Losing our temper
    - Greed: Wanting more than what is required
    - Pride: Over possessiveness
    - Arrogance: One who gives too much importance to oneself
    - Foolhardy: One who is reckless
- Removing these 6 vices, slowly and steadily, with awareness, is a mental model of developing leadership qualities

By acquiring control over one's senses

- We have 5 senses: Sound, Touch, Sight, Taste and Smell
- We understand outside world using these 5 senses through 5 sense organs: Ears, Skin, Eyes, Tongue and Nose
- By controlling these 5 senses, we will restrict the entry of unwanted things into us: INDRIYAJAYA

By cultivating one's intellect by association with elders

- Develop the intellect: by association with elders
- "Elders" does not mean just senior by age but also one who is senior by experience & wisdom: VRIDDHASAIYOGA
- A leader will become a better leader just by associating with wise people (By using the knowledge & wisdom of others, one can develop and cultivate one's intellect)

By keeping watchful eye, using spies

- Spies are informers. Information is the key to success
- Leader should process whatever information gathered, come to the right conclusion & take the right decision
- Be alert & very well informed through a network of spies

By bring about security & well-being through energetic activity

- Primary duty of a leader: ensure security and well-being
- By carrying out necessary activities with full of energy & Enthusiasm / Utsaah: it is key to success of any activity
- Enthusiasm is also contagious. Activities should be full of drive, vigour and passion

By maintaining the observance of special duties by the subjects

- Leader should make sure that others do their general duties (Dharma) and special duties (Swadharma) properly
- Leader (King) has to ensure that the team (subjects) maintain and observe respective duties to keep society together

By carrying out his own duties

- Chanakya gives warning here to leader for his own duties
- 1st step towards successful leadership: Leader should NOT shun his/her own duties: Walk the Talk, Lead by Example
- Be role model for others to follow. Demonstration is the best way of telling other what to do (Then leader automatically gets power to tell others to follow duties)

By acquiring discipline by receiving instructions in the science

- Leader should be self-disciplined person, it leads to success
- One way of doing this is by following the instructions of the experts – from different fields of knowledge
- By gathering knowledge, various possibilities opens up to U

By attaining popularity by association with what is of material advantage

Leader to ensure economic prosperity

- Right way is to ensure development and creation of wealth

- Get associated with the kind of projects that will bring richness to everyone. Encourage entrepreneurship
- By creating such a positive ecosystem, leaders automatically gains popularity

By maintaining proper behaviour by doing what is beneficial

- Leader has to ensure proper behaviour at all times
- Leader is face of the organization / institute / country
- If leader does not behave properly, it impacts the image not only for himself/herself, but the whole body
- Leaders have to be fully aware of their behaviour: in front of others as well as when they are alone
- A popular saying: "The character of a person is judged by how they act not only in front of others, but also when they are in dark all alone"

Administrative Model

- There is a new subject called "Design Thinking", in which we need to mentally design the models we want to create
- When mental design is ready, it is easy to implement
- A framework is required to be created before we start any work – it should be ready structurally in your mind
- Then you can gather the pieces and construct the picture
- Without strong and efficient administrative and secretarial support, a leader cannot be effective
- Efficient leadership includes an efficient administration
- Good administration leads to Good Governance – the key to making people happy
- 3 Key Principles to create Good Administration
    - The Selection of Administrators
    - Testing the Integrity of Administrators
    - Supervision – Key to Administrative Success

A. The Selection of Administrator

- The important decision – that will decide your happiness
- Chanakya during his time created 18 departments for efficient running of the Kingdom

- The Administrative process created by Chanakya may have become outdated with time, but the Principles of Administration never change (In fact with New Technology we can create more efficient Administrative Systems)
- Chanakya in KA Book 1, Chapter 8, Verses 28-29 says:

"From the capacity for doing work is the ability of a person judged. And in accordance with their ability, by suitable distributing ranks among ministers and assigning place, time and work (to them), he should appoint these ministers."

- The king is dependent on his government machinery, (Ministers) which runs the kingdom on a daily basis
- These administrators have to be selected carefully
- What are the criteria? "The ability of an administrator is judged by his capacity to do work"
- You notice some lazy administrators who focus only on paper work / not having enthusiasm / obsessed with red tap – other people get discouraged due to them
- Reverse the scenario – You get motivated / do your best
- A person good at job will be given more work: Law of Nature
- They also create new work – due to enthusiasm and energy
- If one can manage multiple projects, select them as an Administrator
- According to their ability, they should be given the required rank and designation
- A good leader will know the capacity of each of his team member and will give the work accordingly
- A leader has to ensure capable persons are given the right designations (ranks) – so they will feel empowered and work enthusiastically
- The place of their posting is also equally important. High performing officials are underutilized if posted in some remote areas – it's like punishment to them
- When these high performing officials are posted in Capital city / Important HQ reporting to higher authority, they can create wonders – deliver results consistently
- They have to be given time frame for projects. Goal-setting exercise is helpful. When Leader and such Admin person work in "Mission Mode", achieve amazing results

As Patanjali, the Great Yoga Rishi said ….

"When you are inspired by some great purpose, some extraordinary project, all your thoughts break their bonds: Your mind transcends limitations, your consciousness expands in every direction and you find yourself in a new, great and wonderful world. Dormant forces, faculties and talents become alive, and you discover yourself to be a great person by far than you ever dreamed yourself to be."

- When we work with deadline, everything just falls into place. Delays stand out as a waste of time
- Leaders, therefore, work on timelines
- Time is important in Administration. Be punctual, do not delay the matters, take decisions promptly
- Find a purpose in your life – as Time is Limited
- Swami Chinmayananda said, "A single idea can transform a listless soul into a towering leader among men."
- So while looking out for an "Ideal Administrator" , find people with purpose / or you given them a purpose
- Look for above qualities and appoint the Administrator for the right job or rank at the right time and right place
- This will ensure happiness to the Leader as well as his Administrators

B. Testing the Integrity of Administrator

- Corruption is directly linked to leadership and administration – bound to be leakages in the system
- Whole society will have to bear the consequences
- Financial corruption is only one among the many forms
- Corruption can be at
    - Moral Level
    - In the form of supporting the wrong person
    - In the form of wanting to be known as a Good Person
- Administrator has to have highest level of integrity
- Most capable Administrators could be a biggest danger to the country….. Warning from Chanakya
- Administrator may show impressive performance initially, once he is accepted in the system, slowly may turn over confident & begin to believe he can do whatever he want

- 86% of internal frauds in organization are perpetrated by people in Senior Management Position… Study Report
- Hence, in KA Book 1. Chapter 10, Verse 1, Chanakya warns

"After appointing ministers (and administrators) to ordinary offices in consultation with the councilors and chaplains, he should test their integrity by means of secrete tests."

- Appoint administrator / minister first in ordinary office – give a minor tasks: Follow scientific process of recruitment / HR
- Appointment is done in consultation with the councilors, chaplains as well as Raj Purohit who used to check the horoscope of the person
- After appointment, conduct some secret tests to confirm his / her integrity – some sort of Probationary Period = Some calls it Interns, Management Trainee, Temporary
- During this period the leader keep a close watch on the new employee (Period can be 3 months or more)
- There are 4 tests of Integrity:
    - The Test of Loyalty
    - The Test of Material Gain
    - The Test of Lust
    - The Test of Fear
- These tests are conducted without knowledge of that person who is being tested
- Chanakya in KA Book 1, Chapter 10, Section 6 explains:

"Ascertainment of the Integrity of Ministers by Means of Secret Tests" – by dedicating this entire topic

- For those who are in the job of recruiting people in organizations, especially for Senior Management positions
- After passing all these tests, the appointed Administrator can be confirmed as permanent employee and can become part of King's / CEO's core team

1. **The Test of Loyalty**: A colleague of his (sent by system) says something along the lines of "The King is bad, if we can destroy him, both of us can rise to power quickly"

   If the person agrees, it means he is not loyal

   If he rejects such an offer, he passed the test of loyalty

2. **The Test of Material Gain**: A spy in disguise is sent

   He will try to bribe this person: 'You are in such a big organization in such a high post. Kindly do this work for me & you will get this benefit in return

   If the person takes the bribe – he is potential threat

   If he disagree immediately, he can be trusted with financial transactions

3. **The Test of Lust**: Sexual harassment at workplace

   Administrator being powerful person may misuse his power in return for sexual favours. System sends offer

   If the person agrees, then he has failed the test of lust

   If not, he can be trusted in this aspect

4. **The Test of Fear**: Whether person fears death? How he would behave when death approaches? Real Integrity

   A situation is created where this new person is caught and threatened to death. Then he is told 'The only way to escape death is to kill the King': we have plan, join us

   If he agrees, he is disloyal. If he disagrees, it is guarantee that even in worst situation he will not go against king

C. Supervision – Key to Administrative Success

- "The mind is flow of thoughts", said Swami Chinmayananda
- Nothings is constant but mind is the most inconstant
- A person is what his thoughts are! Chanakya – A master psychologist, understood the Human Mind - Depending on mental capacity, he would assign tasks
- We don't work with people but with people's mind***
- The mind can trap you but can also liberate you
- "The mind is your friend & your enemy", Krishna in Bhagwat Gita
- If we know how to use our mind, we can succeed in anything that we do. Life is nothing but a mental game - Understand the Mind and enjoy the Game
- Chanakya never trusted anyone's mind as human mind is inconstant. Hence he kept an eye on King and his Ministers
- His administrative set-up had many checks and balances
- He had spies and he had spies who spied on the spies

- Chanakya in KA Book 2, Chapter 9, Verse 2-4 advices to a leader to set up a good administrative system as….

  "The leader should be constantly hold an inspection of their works, men being inconstant in their minds. For, men being of a nature similar to that of horses, change when employed in works. Therefore, he should be cognizant of the workers, the office, the place, the time, the work to be done, the outlay and the profit of these undertakings."

- This is a profound piece of advice, given by a man who was a psychologist, mind reader and task master

Constantly hold as inspection of their work: *CONSTANT*

- If regular inspection and reviews are not carried out, the people working under you may slip up
- Supervision: an important aspect of good administration
- Providing Standard Operating Procedures (SOPs)
- Management Information System (MIS): quite popular
- Another type: Surprise Checks / Sudden Quiz. So people will remain alert and vigilant and always remain prepared

Men being inconstant in their minds: *Inconstant Mind*

- While doing work, there are chances of losing the focus
- We may lose direction and purpose – Leader's main job is to give direction and make sure team is on the right track
- The journey may be long and tiring – but purpose will keep us going in the right direction

Men, being of a nature similar to that of horses, change mind when employed: Horse - *Strong but Loyal Animal*

- Good horse trainer knows how to tame a wild horse
- Chanakya here compares the mind to horses. When told to do something, everyone initially resists. But if mind is tamed and brought under control, it can do wonders

Therefore, one should be cognizant of the worker, the office, the place, the time, the work to be done, the outlay: Leader: *Be aware of the Workers & Administrators*

- Keep eye on the office, the place of work, the timing of work, the work to be completed and also the expenditure

- Keeping track of workers entry and exit from work premises
- Set up Goals & Key Result Areas (KRAs): For employees to focus on

Profits of these undertakings: *Chanakya meant Business*

- He will always focus on the Return on Investment (ROI) as far as his people and administrators were concerned
- A leader should understand Financial Excellence along with People Excellence (Financial Success is Ultimate Aim)

The Leadership Concept - VIJIGISHU

- Chanakya refers to the leader as Vijigishu, meaning one who wants to be victorious and conquer in spite of the challenges
- Leader has to think like a conqueror and succeed, irrespective of the circumstances
- Leader initially referred to the King of a Country by Chanakya - Today we have leaders in every field: Politics, Business, Science, Academics, Administration, Armed Forces, Society, Community, Various Unions, Sports Teams and even Spirituality
- Some Leaders are great orators and public speakers; while others sit quietly at their desk / laboratory and become "Thought Leaders": give new direction and perspective to the way people think
- Some Leaders are immensely popular when they are alive, their work attains speed and recognition in that generation; some Leaders are celebrated after they are dead, because they were much ahead of their times and their generations could not understand their greatness
- Some Leaders have large following; others may not. Some Leaders are known in particular region while others gain worldwide recognition
- Yet, all these leaders have something in common that gives them respect and appreciation : twhich is nothing but the Attributes of Leadership
- So to become the VIJIGISHU and to Conquer the World, Leader should be RAJARISHI (Sage like King / Leader) following the ....
  - Aanvikshiki : Use the Art of Thinking
  - Swadharma : Following his / her duties perfectly
  - Vruddhasaiyoga : Association with Elders
  - Indriyajaya : Control your Senses
  - Dinacharya : Follow the Daily Routine
  - Saptang Model : Apply in day to day activities for Successful Life

Chanakya's 7 Pillars of Leadership / Saptang Model

- Chanakya describes this leadership model in Book 6, Chapter 1, Verse 1 of the Arthashastra ....

***"Swami, Amatya, Janapada, Durg, Kosha, Dand, Mitra iti Prakritya"* (6.1.1)**

(The King, the Minister, the County, the Fortified City, the Treasury, the Army and the Ally are the constituent elements of the state)

	The Secret	Represents	Today in an Organization
1.	Swami	The King (The Leader)	Owner / MD
2.	Amatya	The Minister (King's Advisors, Councilors)	The Manager / CEO / VP
3.	Janapada	The Country (The Citizens)	Marketing / Customers
4.	Durg	The Fort (Housing)	Infrastructure
5.	Kosha	The Treasury (Money)	Finance
6.	Dand	The Army (The Team)	Team Work
7.	Mitra	The Ally (The Friends)	Consultants / Mentors

A Happy Kingdom consist of

- An ideal King (Swami) as a Leader
- Guided by able Ministers (Amatyas)
- Who takes care of the Citizens (Janapada)
- Providing them Good Infrastructure & Facilities (Durg)
- Making sure the Treasury (Kosha) of the State and the People is always Full
- Which is protected by an able Army (Dand)
- And Helped by Good Allies (Mitra)
- This model gives us a Big Picture of Leadership!

1. SWAMI - The Leader

- Who is a Leader? Why Chanakya places so much emphasis on Leader?

  One may get a Leadership chair (position) by heredity, power or influence. But if one is not Capable, the Chair will not keep you! .... Swami Chinamayanand

- Let's discuss...
  - Which would you choose: A Good Leader or Bad Leader?
  - Which would you choose: A Bad Leader or No Leader?
  - What if the Bad Leader becomes a Good Leader? - Is it possible??

- In Book 1. Chapter 19, Verses 1-5 of the Arthashastra, Chanakya says ….

  "If the King is Energetic, his subject will be Energetic. If he is Slack (and Lazy in performing his Duties) the subjects will also be Lazy, and thereby eat into his Wealth. Besides, a Lazy King will easily fall into the hands of the Enemies. Therefore, the King should himself always be Energetic"
- Leaders set an example and become Role Models
- Bhagvad Gita, Krishna says "As the Leader, so the People"
- Leader must be Physically Energetic, Mentally Alert and Vigilant

SWAMI : Leadership Qualities

- Qualities are not birthrights; they must be developed by hard work and consistent efforts
- These qualities are Universal Principles of Leadership and to become effective Leader you have to practice these Qualities
- Qualities of a Swamy (Leader) are (Book 6, Chapter 1, Verse 3 of KA) …..
  - Intelligent and Dynamic
  - Associate with Elders
  - Truthful in Speech
  - Does not break promises
  - Grateful
  - Desirous of Training
  - Easily Approachable

Swamy: Intelligence and Dynamic

- Two Sides of the same coin
- One can become more intelligent by making an effort to stretch your mind and intellect
- Education must be a continuous and lifelong process
- Reading books, newspaper, research journals helps in making you more aware and informed about the world
- Gathering information does not make you intelligent, you need to develop the skill of analyzing the gathered info, take important decisions and act on those decisions
- Be Dynamic: implement your findings – it requires initiative, guts and self confidence to implement your plans – You have to do that to prove your leadership ability

- Implementing plan is not easy. Great Leaders start and make sure they succeed, in spite of the problems

Swamy: Associate with Elders

- Sanskrit word for this is VriddhaSanyoga
- Means learning from "real-life" experts in filed such as
- Leadership
- Management
- Finance
- Your journey to meet and learn from real-life experts should go on forever
- There are three types of people
- Those who learn from their own mistakes
- Those who never learn from their mistakes
- Those who learn from Other's mistakes (Best One)
- Association with Elders means learning from those who are more mature and experienced than you are
- To keep learning is a great quality of a Leader

Swamy: Truthful in Speech

- Speaking the Truth is very important for a Leader
- One step before that is "Understand the Truth"
- Leader has to find out the Truth before taking any decision
- A Leader should say what he feels is right and correct
- A Leader needs to face reality and the truth is sometimes bitter, but to stand by the side of truth is Leadership
- A Leader needs to remember that "One needs to understand emotions but not get emotional"
- A Leader should let the head rule the heart & not the other way
- "Gut Feel" is a mix of head & heart – the highest level of leadership when one operates from being intuitive
- Intuition comes from insights. Insights comes from understanding the truth
- Only the men of Truth & Integrity prove to be Real Leaders

Swamy: Does not break promises

- Lord Rama: Indian tradition regarded as Ideal King
- Tulsi Ramayana famous couplet about tradition of leadership in Rama's dynasty: "Raghukul reet sada chali aayi, Pran jaaye per vachan na jaayi" : Raghu Dynasty: Even if we need to sacrifice our lives, we will not break our promise
- Leadership is not about over-promising and under-delivering but it is about delivering what is promised
- Walk the Talk: is the mantra: Very Simple, Yet Profound
- Leadership is making people walk on water….It is making them ready for sacrifice….. Narayan Murthy in Chanakya Speaks
- When the world stops…..the leader starts walking…..walk alone….. Nobel Laureate Rabindranath Tagore in Geetanjali
- It was not the promise that you make to others that you have to keep, but the oath you took when you started the journey

Swamy: Grateful

- Gratefulness means humility, where true strength lies
- Powerful people are humble
- Giving credit to team members, appreciating someone will only add to your value
- How do you know if you are truly humble?
- You will have obtained humility when you can no longer find anyone that you think is lower than you in any way
- Everyone may not be equal in power, status or wealth. But the day you realizes that everyone is equal in the eyes of God ….. …… The Leader in you is born

Swamy: Desirous of Training

- Two aspects: The desire to get trained and training others
- Training is very important part of our lives
- Born – Parents – School – Professional Course – Build Competencies – Till this stage we are in high learning mode
- Take job / Profession – settled: we become complacent
- One has to develop attitude of continuous learning

- Push yourself for more knowledge in your respective field
- Secret of success is not just to learn, but to unlearn, relearn and continuously learn
- Learn from books, people, reports, newspapers, Govt. data
- Never keep your knowledge to yourself, share with others
- Knowledge grows when it is shared
- Great leaders build good training systems & institutions
- They design the training programs and invite best people to share their knowledge and wisdom

Swamy: Easily Approachable

- Leader makes himself available to the people when they require him, not just when he requires them
- Leader plays multiple roles: father/mother, friend, philosopher, guide
- Leader is like ready & available resource for any problem
- People look upon him with hope
- Giving unrestricted entrance to people / open door policy is important : it helps for information / data to come to you at initial stages itself
- Olden days, Kings used to have Janata Darbar – a place where king used to meet the common man – Create one for you
- Problem can be handled well in a nascent stage, if decisions are not taken then, it becomes uncontrollable
- Be a problem solver and quick decision maker
- Then the Leader in you starts helping others in the true sense

Swamy - Practicing the Leadership Qualities

- All these qualities are interconnected and signify the various dimensions of a Leader – so where to start?
- Start by practicing any of these qualities – all will slowly develop on their own: Important is to start "Practicing"
- If you start reading more, you become more informed & intelligent – so start looking at things differently – become humble in attitude
- Want to start with grateful – start with open door policy
- To become a Leader – one has to Think like a Leader => for that one has to Act like a Leader => for that it has to come from the Heart
- Let the Leader in each one of you awaken

Swamy - Keys to Leadership

1. Boost the morale of your people. They will look upon you for that
2. Think out of the box. Be ready to experiment
3. Have high moral standards. Personal integrity is the key
4. Give resources to people. Money, tools and techniques are required for every operation
5. Admire mistakes. Do not try to cover them up

2. AMATYA - The Minister

- Who is a Amatya? Chanakya repeatedly emphasized the importance of a Minister in Chapter 8 of Book 1 of KA titled Amatya Utpatti
- Amatya is also called as Mantri or Minister / Manager
- Depending on context, every Leader is a Manager for someone and every Manager is a Leader for someone else
- Example: The CEO of a Company is Leader, while Vice President becomes the Manager / Minister for him. But VP is also a Leader to his Team Members. Similarly CEO is a Manager for The Chairman of the Company
- Why King requires his Amatyas or why Companies require Managers?
- In Book 1, Chapter 7, Verse 9 of the Kautilya's Arthashastra, Chanakya says,

"Rulership can be successfully carried out (only) with the help of associates. One wheel alone does not turn. Therefore, he (the Ruler) should appoint Ministers and listen to their opinion"

The help of associates

- One wheel alone does not turn
- Appoint Ministers
- Listen to their opinion
- The Help of Associates:
- King has to manage whole kingdom
- Leaders know the importance of teamwork
- In olden days King used to have strong associates in the form of his friends, advisors, teachers, mentors and seniors
- In India we have concept of the King being advices by his Gurus

One wheel alone does not turn

- Analogy: If only one wheel to bullock cart, it keeps going in circles
- There is movement but no progress / action but no direction
- Vehicles have to carry heavy cargo
- Bigger the vehicle, more the wheels and stronger they should be

Appoint Ministers

- Number of ministers required depends on the size of the kingdom
- Volume of responsibilities the King handles
- First generation businessmen sometimes do not understand the difference between owning & managing a business
- Owner needs to think about business expansion, potential business opportunities, cost minimization, sources of man power supply, customer satisfaction, profit maximization, etc.
- Hence appoint a Manager who takes care of the details of day to day business operations and frees the owner for "Thinking Time"
- For this Trust people / Manager and delegate him responsibilities
- Make sure you consider Manager as equal: Be grateful to your team and treat them with respect

Listen to their opinion

- Listening is different from hearing – it is an open minded approach towards the other person while he is speaking
- Give yourself challenge to be ready to understand other person
- You open your mind to different possibilities
- Managers also think continuously and apply their minds to the job
- Have hold over ground realities: Swamy's eyes & ears in organization
- Their experience is useless if you do not "listen" to their opinion
- Today's world is one of new ideas and innovation
- A king is as good as the advice he gets. In today's situation, you need to take inputs from your people before taking decision
- Managers help you to think from different perspectives
- Swamy & Amatya are interdependent and their mutual trust is the push required to achieve results

Management?

- Kautilya's Arthashastra in Book 1, Chapter 15, Verse 42 .....

  "The means of staring undertakings, the excellence of men and material (suitable) apportionment of place and time, provision against failure, (and) accomplishment of work – this is deliberation (management) in its five aspects"

- In this one-liner Chanakya defines the 5 Principles of Management:
  - The means of staring undertakings (Assignments / Projects)
  - Excellence of men and material
  - Suitable place and time
  - Provision against failure
  - Accomplishment of work
- These are the basic foundations on which we evaluate...
  - The efficiency of the Manager
  - The productivity of the Organization
  - Its success in achieving Objectives

Let us look at each of these 5 Principles of Management .....

The means of Starting Undertakings

- Need of organization is to manage and complete the projects
- Best Manager is one who not only takes up projects given by his supervisor but also creates projects on his own
- Stephen Covey (Author of "The Seven Habits of Highly Effective People") describe this as being "Proactive" – an important quality for a good Leader and Manager

Excellence of Men and Material

- Manager has access to resources, which can be used at his discretion in order to accomplish tasks / projects
- People work under his directions and his team uses the tools
- Good Manager must be able to make his team highly productive and ensure optimum utilization of material (machinery, budget, etc.)

Suitable Place and Time

- Management is all about deciding the right place and the right time to make your move

- In warfare, timing is very critical (When to attack the enemy)
- It requires careful planning, analysis and also patience
- This sense of right "timing" come from one's own experience, knowledge and guidance from other sources

Provision against Failure

- Every move has to be carefully planned taking two alternatives into consideration: The best scenario of Success and The worst scenario of Total Failure
- Have backup plan, be prepared with alternative solutions
- Consider failures at each stage, plan alternative moves before starting the venture – Have Plan A, Plan B & Plan C in place

Accomplishment of Work

- Management is about achieving desired results
- Have parameters to check have you achieved what you set out to do
- Every project is started with certain objectives and process in mind
- Process may evolve, route taken may change during execution, but target has to be achieved in given time frame

The Professional Man

- The professional man is in essence, one who provides service. It is a service that wells up the entire complex of his personality. In a very real sense, his professional service cannot be separate from his personal being. He has no goods to sell, no land to till, his only asset is himself
- If he does not contain the quality of integrity, he is worthless. If he does, he is priceless. The value is either nothing or it is infinite
- So, do not try to set a price on yourselves. Do not debase yourselves by equating your souls to what they will bring in the market
- Like love, talent is useful only in its expenditure and is never exhausted
- Set the price on your service. But, never confuse the performance, which is great, with the compensation, be it money, power or fame .... Judge Elbert P. Tuttle

Qualities of a Good Manager

- In KA: Book 6, Chapter 1, Verse 4-6, Chanakya states the qualities of an Amatya:

- Desire to Learn
- Power of Retention
- Thorough Understanding
- Intentness on Truth
- Ability to Lead an Army
- Sweetness of Speech

Qualities of a Good Manager

Desire to Learn

- Without continuous learning , there is stagnation in a Manager's career and boredom sets in
- One should forget the difference between weekdays and weekends as every day is a celebration because every day you are learning something new
- One must hate the days when he/she has no work to do
- Manager can also achieve this if work is not considered as "Task" to be completed, but an opportunity to learn
- This is true not only for Owners but for professionals & managers
- They work hard and learn a lot by reading, meetings, travelling, resolving a problem in the company, draw on the experience of seniors, juniors, families, friends, children and their mentors
- The whole universe becomes their University and in that state of mind they become deep thinkers, meditative in nature and are able to find solutions to complex problems

Power of Retention

- What is the greatest problem in our life? – Not being able to remember and apply the knowledge you have when the time comes
- Curse given to Karna by his Guru Parshurama in Mahabharata
- Result: Arjuna who was less skilled than Karna, killed him
- To retain knowledge and recollect it when it is "really" required is a skill a Manager has to develop
- Retention is not just memory skills or reproducing what you have learnt
- It is going into your past database, selecting what one really required, diagnosing the current problem, choosing what is relevant and making the action plan in the shortest possible time

- Have you ever faced an instance in your life when you were all alone in a very difficult situation & took decision in that moment?
- Retention is wisdom in action, no reference or consulting time, no brain storming activity possible. Only you and the moment of truth

Thorough Understanding

- Understanding has to be thorough and complete
- Young lovers often says "I Love U" but these are superficial words
- Real love come from understanding one another completely
- In old couples – you find perfect mental tuning between the two
- There should be thorough understanding between the Leader and the Manager: comes after working together for long period
- When the understanding reaches maturity: No communication gaps or complaints – only a deep sense of calmness
- They work together for higher purpose / achieve common goal
- They may disagree on the methods / have different points of view, but their objective is not forgotten
- If the King & Amatya agree on the same thing, then one is redundant .... Santrupt Misra from Aditya Birla Group
- Strength lies in differences not similarities ... Stephen Covey

Intentness on Truth

- A true Manager will try to understand this complete Truth
- Truth has various dimensions (Story of an elephant)
- It required the wisdom of a person with full vision to see the complete truth
- Manager needs to develop this "Big Picture" vision
- Many people will provide different perspective to a given problem
- He needs to gather all information and collate it into a large story
- In this process, the truth is discovered
- Good Manager have to be aware of and respect the perspective of different individuals but his intentness has to be on the truth
- Means the ability to take the next step – certain action is required after arriving at the truth – One needs to implement his/her findings

- Example: Mahatma Gandhi: Non-violence was the way to freedom – he demonstrated his "Experiments with Truth"

Ability to Lead an Army

- Minister has to ensure that his team implements the King's decision, but for that team members has to accept minister as their leader – hence Minister / Manager has to be inspiring leader
- Leadership is never demanded but commanded
- Authority should never be imposed, people should accept it voluntarily
- Your team should be mesmerized to your vision and ready to do anything at your command
- Be the manager who has ability to lead a team like an army fired up to take up any challenge
- This is Charismatic / Transformational Leadership
- The Manager in you has to transform into a Leader

Sweetness of Speech

- It does not mean being nice to everyone / uniformly sweet
- It is important to keep it simple, communicate complex problem in simple manner
- Manager is the bridge between the senior management and the staff – has responsibility to convey the organisation's need to the last man – to connect each person with vision of organisation
- Similarly he also conveys problems of the staff to management
- Making your team happy is an essential part of management and leadership
- Truth is important, but the ability to communicate the truth in a palatable way is more important
- Be good communicator

Amatya - Tips for Good Management

1. **Be prepared for change:** Never resist new assignments or projects
2. **Manage yourself first:** Self management is important for managing others
3. **Ensure good administration:** Systems and processes should be in place
4. **Know people by name:** It provides the personal touch
5. **Empower people:** Encourage your subordinates to take decisions

3. JANAPADA - The Country - The Citizens / Customers

- Good Governance: Till the last man in the last village is not happy, the work of the government is not done
- There are 2 categories of people in this world who are not blessed with personal happiness: The King & The Teacher
- Till every person in the kingdom is not happy, both cannot take rest
- So Leaders – no personal life
- The King & The Guru are supposed to dedicate their life to the welfare of society
- Work-Life balance: Leader should not differentiate between two
- Personal integrity is important in all spheres of life
- Leadership to be practiced 24 x 7 x 365, it is a lifelong commitment
- Leader will have personal life but cannot be hidden from public eye
- Leader sets an example; he becomes role model
- Yatha Raja Tatha Praja: As the Leader, so the Citizens
- JANAPADA: are the citizens of the country without whom kingdom is not complete
- In today's corporate world, Janapada refers to customers / clients – "The Customer is King", serve them well
- "A customer is the most important visitor on our premises. He is not dependent on us. We are dependent on him. He is not an interruption in our work. He is the purpose of it. He is not outsider in our business. He is part of it. We are not doing favor be serving him. He is doing us a favor by giving us an opportunity to do so." …….. Mahatma Gandhi
- Most companies today have customer services department
- Today after-sales service is a more important component
- Retaining customers have become a big challenge
- Leader should remain in touch with customers regularly
- Think like customer to be a good market leader in your business
- In governance, challenge is to understand how citizens think – try to understand their likes, dislikes, habits, culture, value systems, needs & aspirations and give what they need
- Understand the psychology of citizens / customers
- "The King should be focused on his subjects, not the throne. If the subjects don't exist, the throne will also not exist." Bhishma advises Yudhisthira on Good Governance in Mahabharata

- In Book 1, Chapter 19, Verse 34 of the Kautilya's Arthashastra, Chanakya says:

  "In the happiness of the subjects lies the happiness of the king, and what is beneficial to the subjects is his own benefit. What is dear to himself is not beneficial to the king, but what is dear to the subjects is beneficial to him."
- All marketing theories or principles of good governance will find their culmination in this powerful saying
- This is most quoted and well-accepted theory of Chanakya
- In the happiness of the people is the happiness of the king

Happiness of Subjects

- To be happy is great human achievement
- Entire world including UN trying to understand meaning of happiness to citizens
- Happiness has various dimensions: Physical, Mental & Spiritual

Physical

- If not physically fit / unwell – happiness is far from your mind
- "Health is Wealth" : WHO aims for happiness for every citizen
- Next – availability of adequate food and water
- Also requires bodily comforts / conducive external environment
- Comforts at the physical level can be misunderstood as real happiness
- "You can be in luxury yet unhappy – luxuriously unhappy" ...... Swami Chinmayananda Hence next aspect is Mental Happiness

Mental

- Leader should understand that human beings have sentiments and feelings and need to be emotionally taken care of
- Leader needs to develop Emotional Intelligence
- Increase stress levels in modern living are result of being mentally unhealthy – needs to be taken care of at right time
- Creating a caring and accepting atmosphere is required
- Leader should create an environment that provides emotional security to team members

- Consider mistakes / failures are learning steps
- Importance to team work rather than one-man show
- Employees to get connected emotionally to organization and the office becomes a second home
- Then they never complain about working extra hours to achieve certain goal

Spiritual

- Highest level of happiness and it is the happiness in the real sense
- External problems do not matter as happiness comes from within
- Spiritual happiness comes from the death of the ego
- But leader should not ignore physical happiness of his team
- Once JRD Tata was asked "Do you want India to be an economic superpower?" he replied "No, I want India to be a Happy Country"
- For India to fearlessly stand on its feet on the world platform, we need to connect to the spiritual foundations of our past
- In leadership too, we need to take the highest leap – towards Spiritual Leadership
- To ensure that India becomes a "Happy Country", leaders have to think about complete happiness for the people including spiritual happiness – the real goal of a person's life

Democratic attitude of the king

- Apart from happiness, Chanakya also refers about Democratic Attitude of the King
- Few countries ruled by a King or Queen & their citizens are happy while many countries have democracy, still citizens are not happy
- India, the largest democracy in the world and having one of the best constitutions of the world, still people are unhappy
- India lacks only one thing: Good Leaders (with right attitude)
- The ability to think big, take bold decisions, encourage creativity & efficiency and a fighting spirit makes a great leader
- Chanakya: "In the happiness of the subjects lies the happiness of the king", while our leaders think of only their happiness
- Leader cannot be selfish nor should impose his ideas as a command or dikkat. He should be empathetic, caring & loving

- Then leader feel the pain and unhappiness of the citizens and work timelessly to find solutions to their problems

Self-interest v/s Subject's interest

- "What is dear to himself is not beneficial to the king".....Chanakya
- Leader has to step out of his comfort zone and take up difficult tasks, looking at the long term benefits of his work
- These tasks may not benefit him personally, but if his people are benefited, he should take them up, irrespective of his personal likes
- "What concerns his subjects is what beneficial to him" adds Chanakya
- No action in the world goes without an impact
- No good work goes unrecognized / No work is big or small
- The attitude with which you work is what ultimately matters
- Treat every customer as the most important customer
- You may not be able to solve every problem, but you can make a difference in the way you handle it
- If a situation has come to you, means God wants you to contribute
- You can create a small ripple that can create a revolution

Qualities of Good Citizens

- In KA: Book 6, Chapter 1, Verse 8, Chanakya defines the qualities that keep the subjects safe & secure:
    - Strong position in centre and frontiers
    - Sustainable in times of distress
    - Easy to protect
    - Providing excellent means of livelihood
    - Capable of bearing taxes and fines

Strong position in centre and frontiers

- Chanakya's war strategy: Story of hot rice
- You never attack centre of kingdom directly / stringent security
- Strategy: attack borders first, eliminate less powerful slowly & steadily and then reach the center
- Protecting the frontiers is more critical as infiltration starts from boarders of the country, have forts at major check points

- Chanakya introduced various check posts, passport, visa systems
- Chanakya created a strong espionage system. Included trained and highly intelligent girls spy network called the Vishkanya
- He also created informer network consisting of eunuchs, beggars, priests, old ladies & community leaders. Information is key strategy
- To keep check on spies, Chanakya created a network of counter-spies. Activity of each spy was observed by another spy
- You should trust people, but don't take trust for granted as no compromise on national security

Sustainable in times of distress

- Natural calamities such as floods, earthquakes, volcanoes and draughts come without notice and wreak havoc on a nation
- Leader has to take into account provision for this during planning
- India has National Disaster Management Authority, New Delhi
- Good Leader is one who is capable of survival in time of distress
- Plan looking at history: Japan-Earthquakes, Odisha-Cyclone/Floods
- Learn from past mistakes and plan your future strategy
- Sustainability is the key word here
- People usually migrate when they have lost faith in the leadership
- Even in times of distress, people will not migrate if they have confidence on their leader – a litmus test for leader
- "When the going get tough, the tough gets going": i.e. Leadership
- Corporate Leaders demonstrate this "Together, we shall win"
- Such leaders uplift people's spirits and show a way out
- They leave a lasting impact for generations to come

Easy to Protect

- Response time has to be quick
- Leader should efficiently protect his people with ease
- Imagine – you dial emergency number and there is no response
- If phone is answered on 1st ring, you feel safe and reassured
- Leaders have to be to their citizens what the mothers are to their children

Providing excellent means of Livelihood

- Ensure employment to everyone is KRA of any Leader / Govt.
- Chanakya refers not just money required for basic survival but excellent means of livelihood – enough money for quality life
- A good and steady income instills confidence in every person
- Paying good salaries is also quality of great leadership
- For citizens to be happy, financial planning is important for the leader and should not be neglected

Capable of bearing taxes and fines

- Taxes and fines are revenue for the government
- This money is used for paying salaries of Govt. employees, defence, education, healthcare, infrastructure, other projects
- It is citizen's duty to pay taxes on time
- Chanakya says: "The person who does not pay taxes brings to himself the sin of the king" (Considered sinful act not to pay taxes)
- Chanakya has balance approach, says taxes and fines should be imposed only to the extent of people's capacity to pay
- Policy to ensure win:win situation – A happy society
- ***The safety and happiness of society are the objects at which all political institutions aim, and to which all such institutions must be sacrificed.*** …..James Madison, 4th US President

THE POLICY (Governance / Corporate): Plays major role in taking care of citizens / customers Chanakya's Theory of ***Sama, Dana, Danda*** and ***Bheda***

- Sama: is using method of discussion and guidance
- Dana: means explaining the benefits
- Danda: means showing the rod (symbol of power & fear) or being strict
- Bheda: means elimination / divide and rule

Janapada - Tips to Keep Citizens / Customers Happy

1. **Connect with People:** If they do not come to you, you should go to them
2. **Use the power of the Media:** It is a great partner for doing good work
3. **Show what you have done:** Your customer / citizens should know about the initiatives you have taken for their security and happiness

4. **Follow an Open-door Policy:** You should be accessible to everyone
5. **Empower Customers / Citizens:** Impart training on your skills

4. DURGA - The Fort - The Infrastructure

- In ancient times, the Durga / Fort had many uses
- Forts were located at strategic points: Mountaintop / Coast
- Some forts were big fortified cities with complete civilization living inside such a durga with boundary wall
- Fortified city had various facilities like water tanks, roads, well-built houses, stores for food grains, drainage systems, market place, temples, and places for recreation, gardens, etc.
- Study of forts: to understand development of civilization
- In KA: Book 8, Chapter 1, Verse 2, Chanakya says
- ***"A calamity of constituent, of a divine or human origin, springs from ill luck or wrong policy"***
- One cannot wait for surprises, be prepared for it in advance
- Need to be very vigilant and alert to unknown possibilities
- Calamites & disasters are of 2 types: Divine & Human origin
- Natural Calamities: floods, earthquakes, storms, droughts
- Disasters of human origin: terrorism, mass murders
- Definition of Durga changes according to nature of business
- CEO/Head Office, Factory including Plant & Machinery, etc.
- Expanded concept of Durga in modern nation: Good roads, flyovers, bridges, ports, airports, commercial structures, etc.
- In today's world infrastructure is not just physical but also digital: computers, internet, mobile / telecommunication
- As a leader ensure world-class infrastructure and invest in the best that is available to meet your needs

Qualities of Good Infrastructure

- First create the blueprint / master plan for desired infra
- It can be either Green Field project: you need to build from scratch or Brown Field project: renovate an existing infra
- Think like designer / architect & ask following questions:

- What kind of look do I want?
- What will people feel about it?
- Have I considered the inputs of others?
- Am I thinking long term while building it?
- Will people resist the change?
- What approvals are required?
- How soon can I make it?
- Think on paper, write down the problems & alternative solutions

Qualities of Good Durga

- In KA: Book 6, Chapter 1, Verse 8, Chanakya says: (Hard Infrastructure)
    - Aesthetically pleasing
    - Beneficial to men
    - At the same time, people, who are also part of the infrastructure of an organization or country, should have the following qualities: (Soft Infrastructure)
    - Dedication to work
    - Loyalty and honesty

Hard Infrastucture

Aesthetically pleasing

- Any infra you build must be pleasing and peaceful
- Should look beautiful and impart a sense of well-being to all
- Select right colours, use good material and classy designs
- Infra should be functional, staff should be polite and should help the staff and visitors achieve their purpose of visit

Beneficial to men

- While building, consider needs of the people who will be using it
- Involve them, understand their problems while making blueprint
- Leader should ensure that workplace is inspiring to him as well as to his subordinates and employees
- Since people spent most of their time in their workplace, infra should make them feel at home / comfortable

Soft Infrastucture

Dedication to work

- After building infra, employ people who are dedicated to work
- Employees should be value based, devoted to company's cause
- Leader should be ethical himself to set example for others
- Devotion is state of mind – dedicate your work to a larger goal, welfare of the organisation and the society at large

Loyalty and honesty

- Earn loyalty of an organisation's employees is an important part of the role of good leader
- Benefit of loyalty can only be seen in the long run
- If you work hard and with sincerity, the rewards will come
- Honesty of intent and purpose should be developed in people
- Loyalty can be easily built when the leader stands with his team like a friend, philosopher and guide during crises

Durga - Tips to Build Good Infrastructure

1. **Build world-class facilities:** Do not compromise. Take up the challenge
2. **Focus on hard and soft infrastructure:** Create an environment which is classy
3. **Take other's help:** With inputs from others, you can make it better and faster
4. **Your vision should continue:** If you have seen the benefit of creating something, make it for others as well
5. **Create landmark projects:** In the problem itself lies the solution

5. KOSHA - The Treasury - The Finance

- Kosha as the treasury that keeps the kingdom going
- Chanakya says: First task of the king is to focus on the acquisition, growth and expansion of the treasury
- Treasury maintains the kingdom and helps in its growth and expansion
- King should have a sound understanding of economics, his first activity in day – checking the accounts of kingdom

- The Koshyadhyaksha / CFO: must bring in daily reports and inform the king about kingdom's financial situation
- Artha is wealth and Shastra is scripture
- Arthashastra itself means the Scripture of Wealth
- Scholars called it a book of economics that covers micro & macro economics, accounting systems, auditing rules, collection of taxes & fines and utilization of public funds
- Misconception: India and Indians don't understand money and economics, in-fact we understand money and wealth like no other culture does: we know it's practical value and limitations
- Why do you think we were the most prosperous nation and a target for invaders from all over the world?
- Arthashastra: Knowledge of Wealth & Wealth of Knowledge
- These principles can be applied to modern-day situations
- Strong and well managed treasury is the heart of organization
- Good economic policies create employment and a conductive environment for the growth of trade, business and entrepreneurship
- Good control & management of the treasury leads to the prosperity of the king, the citizens & the kingdom
- Be "Money-conscious" and not "Money-minded"
- Money conscious (MC) person understand the importance of money and gives the right place and value to it
- Money-minded (MM) person, views the world from a financial perspective. The outlook of suck person is ROI in every project. Their attitude is, "What is in it for me?"
- MM draw their powers from their bank balance, the world for them becomes a deal-making platform
- For MC, money is a resource. They respect money, work on finance, but understand that the vision of any project is more important than the finance itself
- MCs are industrious, risk takers, they work for benefit of society - The leaders and role models who create positive change
- The Arthashastra details a financial model called the Four Stages of Wealth....
  - Wealth Identification
  - Wealth Creation

    - Wealth Management
    - Wealth Distribution
- This model can be applied to an individual or organisation
- These four stages in the journey to understand wealth in all its dimensions
- This is the essence of all finance courses, so let us discuss each stage of wealth

1. Wealth Identification

- The starting point. If you want to be wealthy, you need to research and find out areas of wealth creation, take help
- Following right direction and path is important to reach destination
- Business persons look out for potential expansion opportunities
- Investors identify new sectors and industries for good ROI
- Sales man try to identify new market for products / services
- Students asking teachers for guidance on courses to apply, he is looking for an opportunity to build long-term career
- But simply identifying where the wealth is does not guarantee the wealth is yours
- Identification is first step : Now you have to work on it

2. Wealth Creation

- It is laborious task that requires patience and long-term perspective
- Many times there is self doubt, if you will succeed or not
- This is where self-motivation is important
- Winners never quit and quitters never win
- It will be long and tedious journey, but worth doing it
- We study the lives of successful people, we appreciate the success but forget the hard work they have put in
- There is no shortcut to success
- Once you strike gold, once you have created wealth, the whole world changes

3. Wealth Management

- Once you have overcome the challenge of creating wealth, the new challenge is what to do with the money

- Initially you were chasing money, now money chases you
- Success is relative – it brings many new relatives: people want to associate with you, friends, bankers, financial experts
- You should enjoy the money and success you have earned
- Manage your wealth in such a way that you can sustain it
- You need wealth management with proper planning and good advice, start taking right steps for a brighter future
- Wealth management is equally important like creation
- You need to save, invest and manage your wealth

4. Wealth Distribution

- Chanakya says distribute the wealth you have created
- Give it back to the under privileged. Support a needy person, a start-up entrepreneur, a social cause, an artist, the education of a child, health of an impoverished person
- Without you realizing, need becomes greed: caution
- True social service is helping yourself to evolve spiritually by letting go of your possessions
- Share the secrets of your success with others
- Distribute your wealth out of inner fulfillment and not regret
- Wealth: Goddess Lakshmi – we are the only country in the world which has given money a spiritual form /divine status
- Fulfill your Personal Social Responsibility (PSR) – Spiritual Responsibility
- In KA: Book 2, Chapter 8, Verse 1, Chanakya has given brilliant advice as far as finance is concerned:

  "All undertakings are dependent first on the treasury. Therefore, he (the leader) should look to the treasury first"
- Robert Kiosaki, well-known expert and author on wealth, money and investment advices, "Think about possibilities of how to create that money which is required but you do not have."
- Do your calculations and create a budget
- In KA: Book 6, Chapter 1, Verse 10, Chanakya says, the Kosha should have following qualities:
  - Acquired lawfully by ancestors and oneself

- Able to withstand calamity
- Can be sustained even when there is no income for long time
- KA written 2400 years ago. There have been many changes in financial models, institutions and transaction methods

- Coinage → Currency Notes → Cheque → Plastic Cards → Now Digital Money
- Now with internet: e-banking and mobile banking
- Yet the principles are eternal, constant and time-tested laws

Acquired lawfully by ancestors and oneself

- First principle of money – must be acquired lawfully
- Means earned by paying taxes and not cheating others
- With unethical and unlawfully acquired wealth, you lose your peace of mind
- "Wealth that takes longer to create stays for a longer period" … Ramdeo Agarwal, Financial Wizard
- You may be fortunate enough to inherit the wealth acquired by your ancestors
- Chanakya's advice is to expand the inherited wealth, not reduce it
- Make lot of money, but through the right means

Able to withstand calamity

- Financial ups and downs are part of life
- Hence it is important to plan your finances such that you can withstand calamities
- A futuristic viewpoint, rather than immediate gratification – need to sustain your wealth for the future
- The Indian culture believes in savings
- Saving is first step while investment is the next level
- Money that is left over after taking care of basic needs can be invested – investment is a science in itself
- Successful investors are thinkers who take calculated risk
- Save-Insure –Invest: 3 steps to withstand any crises

Can be sustained even when there is no income for long time

- In life, you may face long periods of misfortune
- Financial wisdom is working hard even if there is no income in the short term, as in long run, the hard work will pay off and good times will return

- Some businesses are seasonal, yet salaries to employees must be paid every month (Diwali: Fireworks, Dresses, Car)
- Long term approach requires patience and financial wisdom
- A businessman should plan 10 years ahead, a politician one generation ahead, and a teacher a century ahead
- Wealth is the product of man's capacity to think…Ayn Rand

Kosha - Tips for Financial Management

1. **Consider multiple sources:** You should be able to raise finance from various sources
2. **Goodwill is important:** Along with goodwill, your personal integrity is important
3. **Work for others:** Invest in projects that will be financially beneficial to everyone
4. **Think long term:** Financial planning should encompass both creation and maintenance
5. **Share your wealth:** Share it with others in your team who would otherwise never got the credit for the team's achievement

6. DAND - The Army - The Team

- Army showcases the power of a country and protects the citizens from external threats
- A trained group of people that is ready to fight any threat
- Appropriate selection and training is important to build strong army
- Similarly commitment and dedication is required from team
- One man cannot fight a battle: it's always team that wins a war
- The leader (Captain) is always given credit for team's success
- But leader should not forget to share credit with team members – That is Real Leadership: Share your success with others
- In team, different people have different mindsets
- When team members are able to think about issues from different angles and perspectives, then there is real debate and progress
- Teamwork begins with the leader. He should understand its importance and instill the values of good teamwork in team
- In a team, each member has different strengths and weaknesses. Leader should be able to understand this and allocate work to each member accordingly

- A good leader is someone who gets work done from people who may not even think they were capable of doing it
- After allocating the work, continuously supervise the team
- Leader can delegate work, but not his responsibility
- If team fails, the leader has to shoulder the responsibility
- Chanakya emphasizes that a leader has to be fully alert and regularly keep track of the work his people are doing
- Today it is achieved through MIS: Management Information System

How does one create a good team of dedicated people?

- First step is selecting the right person who has the requisite qualities and qualifications for that particular job
- Testing the person in the selection process itself is key to success
- Next step is to train the person and give him enough opportunities to learn on the job
- In KA: Book 1, Chapter 5, Verse 6, Chanakya describes how to conduct training:

  "Training and discipline are acquired by accepting the authority of the teachers in the respective fields."

Training

- Creating a good team requires training
- It is for this purpose that organizations have induction programs
- People often find their training days to be among the best in their lives, because of the new skills they learn and because these are carefree days with few responsibilities
- The trainee must focus on the purpose of the training and should not take it casually
- During orientation, trainee may not have any work-related responsibilities, but he should remember that he is preparing for many future responsibilities

Discipline

- There are two kinds of discipline – external and internal
- External discipline is imposed by the teachers and other senior authorities. Trainees have to follow a code of conduct and are penalized if they break the rules

- This external discipline should lead to internal discipline or self-discipline
- Trainee should not require the presence of senior authority or threat of penalties to demonstrate disciplined behavior
- Discipline helps build character, it is aura you carry with you
- Being punctual, dressing well, obeying seniors and not keeping any decisions pending are important aspects of being disciplined.
- Disciplined person is respected everywhere

Accepting the authority of teachers

- Discipline can be difficult or easy to achieve
- Chanakya explains that it is easily achieved by accepting the authority of the teacher – trust his maturity and experience
- There should not be any element of doubt about teacher's knowledge when you are getting trained
- If the trainee begins questioning the trainer's ability at the first stage itself, there is no progress
- This quality of tuning to the teacher is called Shraddha
- It is beautiful inner connection between the teacher and the student (by accepting him as the authority in the field)
- It is an inner transformation in the student when he "tunes" himself to the mental wavelength of the teacher

Respective fields

- Teachers are experts in their "respective fields"
- In today's generation of super-specialization, it is especially important for students to listen to and accept each teacher
- Continuous training is essential in today's times
- Be ever-ready student and learn from every person who comes into your life
- Teamwork can be easily achieved if the leader is focused on training & development (TEAM: Together Each one Achieve More)
- Synergy is seen in good teamwork
- In Teamwork, there is happiness instead of frustration, collaboration rather than competition and acceptance instead of denial

Qualities of a Good Team

- The best way to learn teamwork is to observe nature
    - Flock of birds flying in a V-shaped formation: Long flight
    - Ants: forming a perfect line like a parade: Hard work for food
    - Crows work in team: When sight food, they call other crows
- In human beings, teamwork is best observed in villages
- A village is a perfect unit of harmony and co-existence
- Joint family system in India – example of teamwork
- The running of the house was a collective responsibility
- Joint family system also offers security / no babysitters required
- Teamwork also means acceptance – you need to ignore drawbacks of your team members, look at the positive aspects and move ahead in life: "Together we Succeed"
- In KA: Book 6, Chapter 1, Verse 11, Chanakya describes an ideal qualities team should have:
    - Obedient
    - Not disappointed during marches
    - Able to face challenges
    - Experienced in fighting battles
    - Skilled in war and weapons
    - Has no separate self-interest
- If you want to develop good team, develop above qualities in your team. Creating a good team starts with the leader
- A good leader can transform an ordinary team into an efficient team

Obedient

- An ideal team is obedient and accepts the leader's decision
- Team trust the leader's wisdom to take right decision
- If leader is a man of integrity and values, he will look at the big picture and consider everyone's benefit
- Many leaders try to take decisions that will make them popular but leadership is about taking the tough call
- The leader in you will awaken only when you are an obedient follower – Quality of Shraddha (Perfect Obedience)

- Leaders think differently as they have seen and understood the matter much better than us (Wider outlook on big picture)
- Followers have their limitations, hence its better just obey the orders of the leader

Not disappointed during marches

- There are people who run away from troubles
- A team must be ready to march ahead during challenges
- The real test of teamwork is during troubled times
- Bhagavat Gita: psychological counseling of Arjuna (By Krishna)
- When the call comes, you have to get out of your comfort zone, take up your weapons, pray to God to give you strength, stand erect and wait for orders
- Then as the leader instructs, march ahead and give it your best shot. Do not turn back until the battle is won
- Famous saying of Soldier: "Ours is not to make reply, ours is not to reason why, ours is but to do and die"

Able to face challenges

- Entering battlefield does not mean winning the battle
- As you get in, you will find many challenges to overcome
- Team must face the challenges and continue till the goal is achieved – you may need to change strategies to counter the enemy
- It is physically and mentally tiring to face challenges one after another – Leader has to keep inspiring the team
- Either by motivational speech or lead by example
- Inspiration is the fuel that keep a team going
- A good team is comprised of people who set their personal goals aside and focus on what they can contribute to the team's goal

Experienced in fighting battles

- Fighting battles exposes a soldier to real-world challenges
- Practical knowledge is more useful than the theory
- A good team should contain senior, experienced members
- They can share their experience of fighting battles

- Normally 3 generations work together: 1. 50+ years Senior Most, 2. Mid-30s, 3. Fresh recruits in their 20s
- Make sure all 3 generations work in sync with each other
- Experienced members will share their knowledge and wisdom while young lot will bring fresh ideas / new perspectives
- Typical example: computer era - old generation not comfortable with technology and the young lot helping them to learn these skills

Skilled in war and weapons

- No war can be fought without weapons
- The man behind the machine is more important than machine: Team needs to have mix of strategy and resources
- Leader has to ensure that team is given adequate training
- Those who are skilled in war / tactful, should document their ideas and share them with others
- Some people have the ability or knack to get to the heart of the matter immediately – he should help the team
- A good team is one that understands the problem immediately and finds quick solutions

Has no separate self-interest

- All members of the team should be connected to the team's vision (One selfish person can destroy the whole plan)
- A leader should have the ability to pick that rotten apple and eliminate it from the system: before it cause severe damage
- One of the reasons for corruption, is that persons in power forget their responsibilities and misuse the power
- They start taking bribes, so does their team members
- Good teams are formed by people who have the attitude of service to others – called as Seva Bhav
- If we can bring that back in our generation, the future of our nation will be brighter and history will look upon us with price and enthusiasm

Inspiring Your Team
Coming together is a Beginning
Keeping together is Progress
Working together is Success

— Henry Ford

- Creating a Good Team is important for a Leader
- **Akbar** has the **NavRatnas** – the nine gems in his team – his think-tank (Birbal – the Claver Minister & Tansen – Well known Singer)
- **Chatrapati Shivaji Maharaj** had a good team of ministers called **Ashta-Pradhan Mandala** (Core Team of 8 Ministers)

Dand - Tips to Inspire Your Team

1. **Identify your people:** Look for people who are honest and achieve results
2. **Go beyond work:** Team work is inspiring people beyond the work they do in office
3. **Impart training:** Create world-class institutions and training programs
4. **Encourage people:** Organize events, including sports an entertainment
5. **Give credit:** Share successes with your team

7. MITRA - The Ally - The Consultant

- MITRA a word commonly used in all Indian languages, means friend, buddy, colleague or partner
- Even the most powerful king requires Mitra
- He is the friend, philosopher and guide
- You can depend upon him and he is true to you
- He can hold up a mirror and show you what is real
- He is the lighthouse that shows you the way
- He is consultant who offers U the right advice at right time
- This 7th secret can change the dynamics of any game
- A friend can make or break you completely
- Mahabharata: Importance of choosing right advisor at the right time (Remember the incidence) Pandavas won the war due to Krishna's strategic advice at every turn
- An intelligent person is the biggest asset of any team
- Successful companies understand the value of good advisor
- You commit fewer mistakes if you have the best advisors
- A good advisor requires a person who would understand and implement the advice
- Kaun Banega Crorepati: Life Line – Phone a Friend

- Some people hesitate or feel belittled if they have to ask for help – This is disaster – there should not be any ego
- Asking a friend for help can save a lot of trouble
- Friendship is always a win : win situation for both parties
- In friendship, happiness is shared and sorrows are divided
- How does one develop friends? You should be open-minded towards people who come in your life (Read Dale Carnegie Books)
- Chanakya advised leaders to learn from everyone, including children – they are pure, open-minded and truthful
- They sometime gives insights that many adults overlook
- Their opinions are not coloured by selfish desires
- Listening to children is to listen to the voice of God
- A king is as good or bad as his advisors
- Hence leader has to be selective in his choice of advisors and the advice he gets, because the decisions he takes based on the advice can make or break a nation
- Story from Ramayana: Kaikayee wrongly advices by her Dasi Manthara & the crown prince (Rama) was exiled on the day of crowing ceremony for 14 years Vanavaas
- In Arthashastra, various sutras describe the qualities of good consultants and leader's need for good consultants & advisors
- In KA: Book 1, Chapter 15, Verse 2, 35 & 40, Chanakya says:

  "All undertakings should be preceded by consultations. Holding a consultation with only one, he may not be able to reach a decision in difficult matters. With more councilors, it is difficult to reach decisions and maintain secrecy."
- Let's explore this verse further…

All undertakings

- The important word is "ALL"
- All activities (small/big) should be preceded by consultation. Always consult others before you start any project or assignment
- You think along with others and not alone

Holding a consultation with only one

- Single advisor will make you too dependent on that person
- He may guide you, but he may also misguide you

- Good organizations have more than one consultant, as well as more than one vendor and supplier (Way of spreading risk)
- If you have too many advisors, you will get confused
- In KA: Book 1, Chapter 15, Verse 20-21, Chanakya says:

  "Therefore sit and counsel with those who are mature in Intellect."
- We should therefore choose our consultants very carefully

Mature in intellect

- Very important – a consultant to be mature enough
- Consultant can be young in age, yet mature in that particular field
- Example: In the case of cyber crimes, the experts are generally young police officers – as they understand the issues better than most senior officers

Sit and counsel

- Sitting here is symbolic. The term **Upanishad** means sitting below a spiritual master and listening to his wisdom
- Do not just listen to your advisor, discuss the problem with him, ask questions, obtain clarity on the issues concerned
- Time taken out for consultation is very serious affair
- Chanakya days: When one is getting counsel, there should not be any disturbance / it requires secluded space
- Kings were instructed to have a panel of advisors – the council of Ministers – with whom they would spend time daily to discuss the matters of the state
  - Akbar: **NavRatnas**
  - Chatrapati Shivaji Maharaj: **Ashta Pradhan Mandal**
- You will often find businessmen, who are not very qualified but successfully run multinational companies
- The secret of such businessman's success is that his team comprises highly educated and globally experienced people
- They are paid well and taken care of
- Make sure you pay your advisors well. Consultants cannot be valued in terms of money : they are as asset by themselves
- You cannot bargain or negotiate for good advice

- Mahabharata: Remember how Duryodhana took care of Karna
- If you take care of consultants, they will take care of you
- In most cases, Consultant becomes a part of the family and stay along with the organization forever: Truly becomes Mitra

Qualities of Good Ally

- Leaders cannot walk the path alone
- Like anyone else, they too require companions
- Seek friends lifelong. Friendship is about Companionship
- You can learn from various Leadership Styles
- Champions learn from other Champions
- Leaders want to grow: To Learn, Unlearn and Relearn
- Leaders want to share their knowledge and experience
- Once you are in a Leadership Position – it becomes Fun
- It becomes a hobby and game and you require friends to play games – You require like-minded people
- Then life is not just easy, but a continuous learning process
- In KA: Book 6, Chapter 1, Verse 12, Chanakya says while choosing your allies, you should look for some qualities as follows:
    - Alliance from the days of your father / grandfather
    - Greatness
    - Constancy
    - Self-control
    - No separate self-interest
    - Ability to mobilize quickly
    - Begin by being friendly to others. In long run, some friends go out of your life and some stay back as lifelong friends

Alliance from the days of your father / grandfather

- This refers to family friends whom you have known for 2 or 3 generations
- The families know each other very well and have supported each other in difficult times
- One learns the value of friendship in such an environment
- In many cases, marriages take place between families that have been friends for generations

- Children feel comfortable as they have known each other since childhood – there is perfect tuning, easy to adjust
- The longer you know the friend, the better your rapport
- Both know each other's strengths and weaknesses, both know how other person thinks

Greatness

- When two people becomes partners, it's important to respect each other / No two people can think alike
- Focus to discover strengths of other partner
- Your friend should be "great" means that he / she should have qualities that you admire, that you wish to possess
- A person is known by the kind of friends he / she has
- Good friendship is called Satsang in Sanskrit; Company of good, noble and spiritual people
- It is the primary duty of parents to ensure that their children are always in good company
- An average person becomes great by being in company of the great: he imbibes Nobel virtues from his friend

Constancy

- Everyone wants to associate with successful people
- Very few people support you during the struggle for success
- In success, friends know you, and in failure, you know who your friends are
- Hence Chanakya points out that: Friend is to be Constant – in times of struggle, failure and also success
- There is Marathi saying: "Kama purta Mama"
- Good times / Bad times, come and go, but friendship remains forever – Friends are the real asset in your life
- The secret of success for every leader lies in the number of his real friends. This is the asset the leader has to develop during his lifetime

Self-control

- Another test to find out if you have the right friend on your side. He should have self-control

- A person who keeps his mind and senses under control can never go wrong. He will never cross the limit
- He is disciplined, well-mannered and well-behaved
- He has a balance views and does not lose his cool
- Such a person is strong from within
- He control his thoughts, speech and actions when required
- He is not impulsive, thinks through the consequences before act. Such a friend is controlled spender too
- He never gambles, not impulsive, speaks words of wisdom
- He is thinker and doer : He is humility personified

No separate self-interest

- A true Mitra never thinks of his benefit alone
- He thinks win:win – make sure all of you succeed together
- There is no separate / individual interest for him in project
- Friendship can exist among individuals and organizations
- They come together & create a win-win situation for each other. Focus on everyone's benefit rather than individual
- Some organizations also conduct research together
- Business groups come together to form associations
- Dr. Abdul Kalam said, "In the past, leadership style was about competition. Today it is about collaboration"
- Come together, collaborate and think win-win: Formula for Success

Ability to mobilize quickly

- A good associate will be able to come to your aid immediately – an emergency number you can dial
- A true friend will know when you need him, even when you do not tell him – he is mentally attuned to your needs
- In troubled times, such friends can be mobilized quickly
- Brilliant friends are a moral support
- You should also make sure to develop these qualities
- Discover the good friend inside you
- ***"I would rather walk with a friend in the dark, than alone in the light"*** …… Hellen Keller - **an American author, political activist, and lecturer. She was the first deaf-blind person to earn a Bachelor of Arts degree**

MITRA - Tips for Working with Allies & Friends

1. **Network:** It is important to have a good network of friends
2. **Organize meetings:** Gather regular information from your team
3. **Use your intelligence:** It is important to distinguish between right and wrong
4. **Cultivate informers:** They are key to creating strategy
5. **Help your friends:** You need to help your allies when they are in need

HARI OM

References

Aanvikashiki – Art of Thinking by Dr. Radhakrishnan Pillai, Link: https://youtu.be/xdTXyLqoCQs

Above are some selected YouTube Links of Dr. Radhakrishnan Pillai Sir's talks. Interested person can find many small duration clips of Dr. Pillai Sir on various topics of Chanakya on YouTube.

Chanakya & the Art of Getting Rich by Dr. Radhakrishnan Pillai, Link : https://youtu.be/lhjdezt35lY

Chanakya & the Art of Getting Rich by Dr. Radhakrishnan Pillai, Link : https://youtu.be/Un_Y7zg6Frl

Chanakya & Youth of India by Dr. Radhakrishnan Pillai, Link: https://youtu.be/ZgQ2_0JA9M4

Chanakya and Art of Getting Rich by Dr. Radhakrishnan Pillai

Chanakya and the Art of Parenting (at OCLF session) by Dr. Radhakrishnan Pillai, Link: https://youtu.be/_fAfAER3JMA

Chanakya and the Art of War by Dr. Radhakrishnan Pillai

Chanakya in Daily Life by Dr. Radhakrishnan Pillai

Chanakya in You by Dr. Radhakrishnan Pillai

Chanakya in You by Dr. Radhakrishnan Pillai, Link: https://youtu.be/6KPxYh5JpUo

Chanakya Neeti by Dr. Radhakrishnan Pillai

Chanakya Neeti Explained by Dr. Radhakrishnan Pillai – The Ranveer Show, Link: https://youtu.be/hsMN1Pi9Rbs

Chanakya Neeti for Successful Life, Webinar by Dr. Radhakrishnan Pillai, Link: https://youtu.be/LPZ-0dgkME4

Chanakya's 7 Secrets of Leadership (Audio Book) by Dr. Radhakrishnan Pillai, Link: https://youtu.be/FJcnmDrt4Hc

Chanakya's 7 Secrets of Leadership by Dr. Radhakrishnan Pillai and Mr. D. Shivanandhan

Chanakya's Advice for Indian Entrepreneurs (at The Jay Thakkar Show) by Dr. Radhakrishnan Pillai, Link: https://youtu.be/WUpWbFfYvGI

Chanakya's Saptang Model & Leadership, Recording of Live Session with Dr. Radhakrishnan Pillai), Link https://youtube.com/live/bA7Y8tR_JFs?feture =share

Chanakya's Saptang Model (Webinar organised by BIA with Dr. Radhakrishnan Pillai), Link https://youtu.be/tbKjea5-ovM

Chanakya's Wisdom for Happy Life by Dr. Radhakrishnan Pillai, Link: https://youtube.com/live/cg3NZ99wt1o?feature=share

Corporate Chanakya by Dr. Radhakrishnan Pillai

Corporate Chanakya on Management (Audio Book) by Dr. Radhakrishnan Pillai, Link: https://youtu.be/daiZZ2Cth1M

Corporate Leadership (at MA-LS class, CIILS) by Dr. Radhakrishnan Pillai, Link: https://youtu.be/gmTbJAMBCDk

Entrepreneurship Lessons from Chanakya's Life by Dr. Radhakrishnan Pillai, Link: https://youtube.com/live/NrkhPiB3Bs0?feature=share

Financial Concepts in Kautilya's Arthashastra (at MA-LS class, CIILS) by Dr. Radhakrishnan Pillai, Link: https://youtu.be/pbGDFZoFqwA
Grow Your Income 10X by Using Chanakya Neeti (at DBC Podcast) by Dr. Radhakrishnan Pillai, Link: https://youtu.be/NvteVDkMYyQ
How to Start a Business? By Dr. Radhakrishnan Pillai, Link: https://youtu.be/HFsE7rdoONw
Inside Chanakya's Mind – Aanvikshiki and The Art of Thinking by Dr. Radhakrishnan Pillai
Leadership & Management by Author of Corporate Chanakya - Dr. Radhakrishnan Pillai, Link: https://youtube.com/live/MvuKNy6MCeE?feature=share
Leadership Lessons from Chanakya (at 10th Mutual Fund Round Table Conference) by Dr. Radhakrishnan Pillai, Link: https://youtu.be/aq43epVQjrY
Leadership Lessons from Chanakya by Dr. Radhakrishnan Pillai, Link: https://youtu.be/8dKljl7NAo8
Life Lessons from Chanakya by Dr. Radhakrishnan Pillai, Link: https://youtu.be/7d8k9rMtx5U
Secrets of Influencing People – The Chanakya Way by Dr. Radhakrishnan Pillai, Link: https://youtu.be/16vEr_AkJbM
Simplest Indian Way of Finding your Passion (Swadharma) by Dr. Radhakrishnan Pillai, Link: https://youtu.be/w3UuSkMHDbk
The Art of Winning - The Chanakya Way by Dr. Radhakrishnan Pillai
Thus Spoke Chanakya by Dr. Radhakrishnan Pillai
Understanding Chanakya's Mind (at Open Pathshala) by Dr. Radhakrishnan Pillai, Link: https://youtu.be/q97ndm8f6QE
Vijigishu – How to be a World Conqueror (Leader)? By Dr. Radhakrishnan Pillai, Link: https://youtube.com/live/CKv6Tbqewac?feture=share
Winning Strategies by Chanakya for Winners by Dr. Radhakrishnan Pillai, Link: https://youtu.be/FJWoq4cDIPQ